D1237993

White Grizzly Bear's Legacy

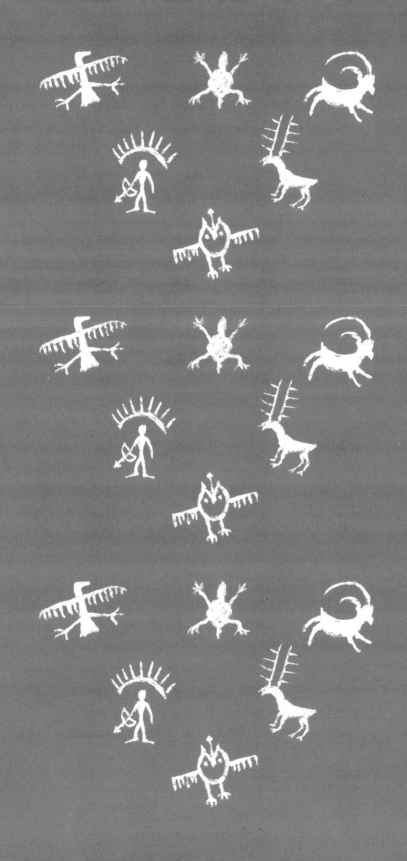

White Grizzly Bear's Legacy

Learning to Be Indian

LAWNEY L. REYES

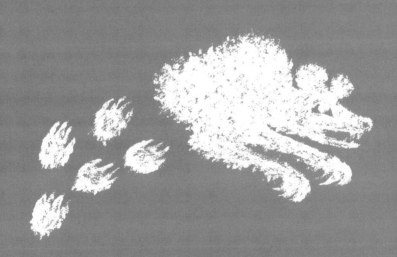

UNIVERSITY OF WASHINGTON PRESS

Seattle and London

White Grizzly Bear's Legacy
is published with the assistance of a grant from the
NAOMI B. PASCAL EDITOR'S ENDOWMENT,
supported through the generosity of Janet and John Creighton,
Patti Knowles, Mary McLellan Williams, and other donors.

Library of Congress Cataloging-in-Publication Data

Reyes, Lawney L.
White Grizzly Bear's Legacy : learning to be Indian / Lawney L. Reyes.
p.   cm.
Includes bibliographical references.
ISBN 0-295-98202-0 (alk. paper)
1. Sin Aikst Indians.   I. Title.
E99.S546R49 2002   979.5'00497—DC21   2001055502

Dedicated to my grandchildren,

Gaby, Recy, and Sebb

Indian People are more than feathers, they are more than paint. They are a deeply humanistic group of people who learned to live within their environment in a way that allowed an understanding of their environment and, therefore, of themselves.

—Richard Milanovich, Agua Caliente Band,
Cahuilla Indians, Palm Springs, California

CONTENTS

CONTENTS

PREFACE

During her lifetime, my mother, Mary, traveled often to the Colville Reservation and to different parts of the country. She looked up old friends who were members of the Lakes Tribe. My mother taped her talks with them. They sometimes exchanged words in Sin-Aikst, the language of our tribe, to recount days past. She visited the National Archives and Records Administration in Seattle several times to learn about Kettle Falls and the tribes that fished there. My mother also consulted the archives in Washington, D.C., to obtain information about the Colville Confederated Tribes.

Over the years, my mother collected substantial information on cassette tapes and in writing. She planned to include what she learned in memoirs about our family, our friends, and our people. The information she gathered included details about the activities and accomplishments of her father, White Grizzly Bear (Pic Ah Kelowna); Chief James Bernard, her uncle; and Chief Kin-Ka-Nawha, the uncle of James Bernard. Further research produced information about Chief See-Whel-Ken, the uncle of Kin-Ka-Nawha.

My mother's goal of writing her memoirs was not realized. On Memorial Day in 1978, she was killed in an automobile accident on I-90, one mile west of the Washington-Idaho border. Two friends of the Lakes

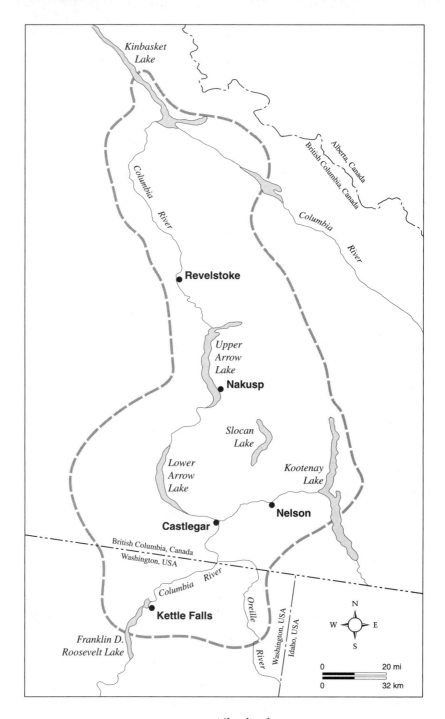

MAP 1. Sin-Aikst land area

Tribe, Lena Laramie and Helen Ferguson, the driver of the car, died with her.

After my mother's passing, I read her assembled notes. As I listened to her cassettes, I began to remember and appreciate a lifestyle that was a part of my heritage, although it was very different from the way I live today. The more I read, the more interested I became.

I talked to family and friends about what my mother had written. Friends who were my mother's age as well as those who were older agreed with her accounts. Here was the story of a people who had lived for centuries in a beautiful part of the Northwest. Their lifestyle, their adventures, and, finally, their demise fascinated me. I realized that, through my family and forebears, I was a part of this.

It seemed important to record and save my mother's memoirs. I thought that our family and those members yet to come would benefit from the information my mother had collected. As far as I know, there is no complete record of the Sin-Aikst Tribe and how they lived. No in-depth written work defines their religion and culture. Some information is available on the loss of their land and how they managed to survive on a reduced land base. But little has been written of their plight after their important food staple, the salmon, was destroyed.

It turned out to be important that my mother had researched people and friends while they were still in good health and remembered the Sin-Aikst traditions. Almost all of them are dead now, and their unique knowledge has died with them. If they had not shared their knowledge with my mother, it would have been impossible for me to carry on her work.

In 1984, I took early retirement from the Seafirst Corporation in Seattle. I wanted to devote my remaining years to painting, sculpture, and travel. My interest in my mother's assembled work was also growing.

After Rebecca Pabrua, my son Darren's wife, gave birth to my first granddaughter, Gaby, and my daughter Lara gave birth to my second granddaughter, Recy, I devoted time to them. I traveled to Walnut Creek, California, to take care of Gaby while her parents worked. Later, I also helped care for Recy, after she was born in Pullman, Washington. They are both beautiful and intelligent children, and they have inherited the beauty of their grandmother, Joyce.

After spending months caring for my granddaughters, I decided to complete my mother's work. I reassembled her notes and put them in order. I wanted to make sure that members of our family understood our relationship to our forebears and to the People as a whole. It was important to me to leave them more than a shallow understanding of our family's past.

As I became more involved, I found questions without answers. More research was required to tie everything together. After much probing, memories of a part of the past came back to me. Visual aspects and landmarks began to appear in my mind like long-lost friends.

Like my mother before me, I traveled to Inchelium and the Kelly Hill area. I talked to old friends who were members of the Lakes Tribe. As we talked, experiences of the past came back to me. Many of my earlier questions were answered. I also received important information about the lives of my grandfather, grandmother, and other members of the family who had lived before them. A woman in Nelson, British Columbia, sent copies of original letters that had been drafted by my grandfather and his mother, Antoinette, requesting the provincial government to turn their land across the Columbia River from Castlegar into a reserve. Copies of newspaper articles about my grandfather and others in the family were also sent to me. This and other information in articles and books gave me a clear picture of my family and the Sin-Aikst Tribe to which we belonged. I began to remember clearly my days at Kettle Falls, the Columbia River, and the town of Old Inchelium. The past came back to me as if it were only yesterday.

I read books of stories about certain parts of the homeland and traditional lifestyle, and studied other books that covered the rituals of birth, death, and spiritual power. As I read, I realized that the completion of Grand Coulee Dam had changed the homeland and the old lifestyle of our people forever. Because of the dam, salmon could no longer reach the falls and their places of origin in the upper Columbia, and a very important source of food was destroyed.

This new information was interesting and provocative. I shared some of my findings with friends, and they were fascinated by my revelations. One mentioned that he had traveled the areas that had been the homeland of the Sin-Aikst. He said he knew the country well from Kettle Falls to north of Revelstoke, B.C., and added that he had wondered more than once about the Indian tribes that lived in the area before the coming of the white man. He said, "A written work about that tribe would be very informative to the people who made their homes in the area. I don't think there are any Indians living there now." Another advised, "Write a book instead of just memoirs about your family." They considered my life unusual and thought that learning about the lives and experiences of my family, forebears, and the Sin-Aikst people would be an enriching and interesting experience for others.

One day, I began writing out in longhand everything I could remember about my family and personal experiences. As I progressed, I realized that I could not tell the story of my family and forebears in depth without including the story of the People, the Sin-Aikst Indians, as a way of binding everything together.

The written work that follows is a concise and chronological telling of events in the lives of my family, my forebears, and the People. It shares intimate passages in our struggle to survive. I am satisfied that my writing will provide my grandchildren, Gaby, Recy, and Sebb, along with others who may come, with an accurate and substantial record of our family's past. A degree of diligence will enable them to understand and appreciate where we have been and what we have been through. I trust that this knowledge will help them understand a little bit about themselves and hope it will enable them to gauge their lives so they might contribute something of value during their own time.

ACKNOWLEDGMENTS

While I was working on the first draft of my manuscript, I knew I had a story. The information collected by my mother proved most important. The stories she shared with me of the Sin-Aikst/Lakes, and our family were invaluable. I learned, however, while working on the manuscript, that I did not know how to write.

My friend Therese Kennedy Johns came to my aid. She taught me how to operate a computer and offered advice on restructuring the manuscript so that everything fell into place. When material did not relate well to the story, she suggested whether to delete or change it. She helped with the wording. Therese bolstered my courage and restored my confidence more than once.

I sent a copy of the manuscript to the Washington State University Press in Pullman. Keith Petersen, the editor, reviewed it and advised that I had achieved my goal in writing a memoir. He added that more work was needed to create a book. He recommended well-written autobiographies that inspired me to learn to write. Joan LaFrance, a longtime friend of our family, shared important thoughts with me. She unraveled the mysteries of writing. Because of her, the manuscript became complete and took the form I was seeking.

After much work, I showed the manuscript to Ron Chew, the director of the Wing Luke Asian Museum in Seattle. Ron called me a month later and said, to my pleasure, that he liked the manuscript. He asked if he could present it to the University of Washington Press in Seattle. He wanted Naomi Pascal, the editor in chief, to review it. Two months later, Ron called again to say that Mrs. Pascal liked the manuscript and was interested in publishing it.

White Grizzly Bear's Legacy

1 / Reflections

Poco and I arrived at Twin Lakes in the late afternoon. We drove the winding dirt road through the heavy forest of pine and fir, stirring a fine cloud of dust. We were en route to my grandfather's property, which bordered the North Twin. As we approached the lake, I remembered the smell and feel of the land and the trees. It was as beautiful as ever. The only movement on the lake was that of fishermen in rowboats quietly fishing for the large rainbow. As we exited the car to walk to the beach, a squirrel high up in a pine tree signaled our approach.

We had been here before, and Poco knew that we were on our land. Poco was a six-pound Maltese, my best friend. We were inseparable. During the last six years, we had traveled half of the United States together, visiting many Indian tribes. We always learned new things about the different cultures as tribal news was shared and met many interesting people from tribes that I had only known from books. Now, back on familiar ground, he systematically re-marked his territory and sniffed at trails made earlier by the inhabitants of the area. We walked to a grass-covered bank above the water. I sat down to smoke a cigarette in the shade of the trees. Poco joined me, and we sat in silence, enjoying everything before us. The wind blowing through the trees above knew us and welcomed our arrival.

As I studied the lake, I thought of the many times my family had assembled and camped here. I remembered the cold of 1935, when our family of four spent the winter. There was much snow, and the lake was frozen over. I was four, and Luana, my sister, was two. I could spot the area on the lake where my dad had cut a hole in the ice to fish for rainbow trout. Luana and I would watch in wonder while our dad caught the hungry fish. As he caught each one, he gave it to me to place in a pile away from the hole. My dad cleaned them and gave them to me. Then I took the fish to my mother, who was preparing dinner in the tent above, where we lived.

My dad and mother loved the lakes and spent much time during the year fishing and hunting there. The clean water was pure enough to drink. The lakes were close to Gold Mountain, and during August we would go up to the summit and pick our supply of huckleberries. When we returned to the lakes, we could have some berries with our meals. The rest we cleaned and dried for future use.

Over the years, we came to Twin Lakes to fish, swim, and go boating. Hunting for deer was also good in the surrounding mountains. We spent much time searching the ravines and deer trails when our meat supply was low. Once a year, almost all of the People who were living in Old Inchelium picnicked at Carson Beach, a mile from my grandfather's property. There, they recounted stories of the good days before the Columbia River rose to cover Kettle Falls and destroyed the great salmon runs. Those were hard but adventurous times, and everyone was occupied cooking over campfires, swimming, boating, and hunting in the ravines near the lakes. Tepees and tents were pitched throughout the area, and the days ended to the rhythm of drums as the People gambled during the stick games.

After walking the trails around the property and inspecting points of interest, I became hungry. I felt like having an early dinner and asked Poco if he was hungry. He growled and wagged his tail.

We drove the forty-eight miles to Barney's, the only restaurant overlooking Lake Roosevelt. The best steaks in the state of Washington are served at Barney's. It was there that my family used to celebrate many evenings by gathering over steaks and cocktails. We reminisced and talked about the old days before the Columbia River rose and covered Kettle Falls. My mother shared stories about her father, Alex Christian (White Grizzly Bear). She told us of his travels and his hunting and fishing adventures. She also talked about the Sin-Aikst Tribe, the tribe that we belonged to, during their good days. We always enjoyed hearing my mother's stories about her father and the tribe.

After I finished dinner, I returned to my car. I could see Poco watching me from inside. His tail was wagging. I opened the door to let him out, then knelt and gave him a part of my steak. I watched as he gulped it down. I poured some water into my cupped hand and offered it to him. Poco always appreciated water offered to him in this way. He lapped it up eagerly. We had gone through this routine many times. It was our ritual of respect and friendship.

I lit a cigarette and walked over to the granite memorial to Chief James Bernard. Bernard was my mother's uncle. He was chief of the Lakes Indians from 1900 to 1935. I read the accomplishments of his life engraved on the back of the memorial. He was the last Lakes chief in the Kettle Falls area. During his lifetime, many in the tribe depended on him and respected him. My mother, too, had expressed much respect for him.

I walked with Poco across the highway and stood on the bank overlooking Lake Roosevelt. My attention was directed to the area where Kettle Falls had once flowed. I remembered the beauty of the falls before it was flooded by the Columbia River when Grand Coulee Dam was completed.

As I stood there, the wind came. When I listened, I imagined it was talking to me. I felt that the spirits of Kettle Falls were telling me how things once had been. I began to think of relatives and friends who were no longer living. They began to appear before me, perched on the large rocks, eagerly fishing for the great salmon. I envisioned the immense tepee encampments of many tribes near the river. I imagined the beauty of Sin-Aikst canoes as they cut through the swift-flowing river above the falls. Thoughts of my Sin-Aikst ancestors, who had camped and fished here throughout the centuries, came to me.

Kettle Falls, as it once was, filled my mind's eye. I could hear the thunderous roar as the churning water worked its way downriver. Mists created by the spray of water billowed, then hovered over the falls, pierced here and there by colorful transparent rainbows. Dragonflies, yellow jackets, and other winged insects continually penetrated the mists.

A variety of birds flew excitedly over the falls. They appeared to ricochet between rock formations exposed by the fast-moving water. Red-tailed hawks circled, then glided lazily with the wind high in the sky above. The chinook, many very large, leaped powerfully, struggling to clear the falls. The shouts of the men as they fished came back to me. Some spoke Sin-Aikst, others English. There was laughter, then praise as the men pulled in their spears, nets, and fish-traps and their prizes of struggling and twisting chinook.

My mother's stories of the People came back to me. Visions of their lifestyle and how they had survived from season to season made me pause in wonder. They had trained dogs to herd deer out of the hills and ravines and down to the banks of the Columbia, where hunters could take them with bows and arrows. Their method of fishing, which allowed many of the large Chinook to escape and spawn in the upper Columbia, seemed thoughtfully planned. Knowledge that enabled the People to locate and select roots and plants for medicine, food, and other practical uses crossed my mind. Memories of the beliefs, legends, and religion of the spirit powers came back to me. I marveled at how basic, and yet how powerful and meaningful, these beliefs had been to my ancestors.

I recalled with deep respect the lifestyle of the People, the Sin-Aikst, and the great adventure of their experiences as they met the challenges of survival. Memories of the old days embraced me. I became a part of the past as I remembered the Way.

2 / The Sin-Aikst

During my early years and later, after I was grown, my mother shared with me stories of the Sin-Aikst, before they were known as Lakes. She told me they were a tribe of about 3,000 people, spread across a large land area in British Columbia along the Columbia River. This area included the northeastern part of Washington State around Kettle River and Kettle Falls.

My mother told me that the Sin-Aikst lived in several bands and were always close to the Columbia and Kettle Rivers. She explained that the Sin-Aikst chose to divide the tribe into bands because it was easier to maneuver smaller numbers of people for hunting and fishing, and these groups could always gather enough roots, plants, and berries to satisfy their needs. Horses, when they became a part of the tribe, were divided among the bands and were able to find adequate grass and feed in smaller numbers. The Upper Sin-Aikst Indians lived around the Arrow Lakes in British Columbia, above Revelstoke and around the Castlegar, Trail, and Slocan Valley area. The Lower Sin-Aikst lived in the Northport, Bossburg, Marcus, and Kettle Falls area in Washington State. The Sin-Aikst Indians were related to the Swhy-ayl-puh (Colville) Indians who made their home in the Colville Valley and at Kettle Falls and the land south of the falls along the Columbia River.

As the years went by, cooperation, friendship, and marriages took place between the two tribes. Their ties were strong, and there was never any dissension or animosity between them. The language of the two tribes was basically the same. They lived in an area that provided them with all they needed. They were content with what they had and did not expect anything more.

I learned from my mother and elders of the Lakes Tribe that our forebears, the Sin-Aikst, lived by strict codes of conduct that had been established and passed down over centuries. The codes of conduct and ways of life were respected and followed by everyone in the tribe.

When the Sin-Aikst discovered spirit powers, they revered them, and as they learned more about them, these powers became the religion of the People. The understandings and beliefs practiced over centuries formed the basis for a system of behavior, honor, and respect within the tribe.

My mother went on to say that the character of a newborn Sin-Aikst was shaped early, while still in the mother's womb. She said the child was influenced by the actions of the mother-to-be and how she lived. Before the baby was born, the mother-to-be engaged in vigorous exercise. She began the day with a bath in the cold water of a stream or river, then prayed to the rising sun for health and a safe delivery. She moved adeptly and quickly so that the baby inside her would not grow up to be lazy. The mother-to-be was active and worked hard all day to teach her baby about the rigors of hard work. She maintained an even temper so that the baby would be good-natured and of good character.

The parents-to-be spent much time together because others in the tribe avoided them while they were in their special state. They went out of their way to avoid all hostile shamans. The possibility that evil spells might harm the baby in some way was understood, and the parents-to-be did their best to avoid them.

They practiced behavior that had been established among the People for centuries. The mother-to-be respected those in the tribe who were crippled or handicapped so that her baby would not be born with the same condition. She avoided looking at rabbits to prevent her baby from developing a harelip. She knew that she must never look upon a corpse, or her baby would be stillborn. Certain animals and birds such as spruce grouse (fool hens) were not eaten, to keep the baby from becoming demented. Bear meat was also not eaten. The parents-to-be did not want to anger other bears that might retaliate by attacking them or the baby.

When the labor pains began, a midwife arrived to help with the birth. She prepared a bed of grass and fir boughs. Four stakes were driven into the ground: two at the head of the bed so the mother-to-be could brace herself by holding on to them during labor, and the other two at the foot of the bed, where she could push her soles against them and force her knees upward. During labor, the mother-to-be did not moan or cry out, knowing that others would criticize her if she did.

Immediately after birth, the cord was tied and cut. The midwife washed and cleaned the baby in a bath of lukewarm water contained in a tightly woven basket. Afterward, she vigorously rubbed the baby's legs and arms in order to form and strengthen them. Then the baby was wrapped tightly in buckskin to make sure he or she would grow tall and straight and would not have bowed legs.

The nose was pinched at the bridge to form it and make it more prominent. It was massaged daily for ten days to produce a high, shapely bridge. The mother stretched and widened the corners of the eyes with her fingers to make the eyes larger. She massaged the face to smooth the skin and make the features even.

The baby's name was not selected until the mother left the menstrual hut and life returned to normal. Grandparents or an older relative named the baby after a deceased ancestor. Later, the name might be changed to honor another person or some being from the forests, mountains, or river.

Baby clothes were made of soft skin such as rabbit that had been tanned with the fur left on. Diapers made of soft buckskin were washed daily. Amulets of wood or bone represented the spirit power for the baby and took the form of a pendant that hung from a buckskin thong around the neck. Playthings for the baby, such as simplified forms of animals, were carved from wood. Dolls were made from wood, buckskin, and human hair and were decorated with beads and designs sketched and painted on the buckskin with vegetable dyes.

Relatives usually made a cradleboard with a buckskin hood for the baby. The cradleboard was made of woven willow or cedar slats bound in a V shape with a rounded top and narrow bottom to fit the baby's body. It was covered with soft buckskin and sometimes decorated with woven porcupine quills or beads and other trinkets. The hood was tied securely to bind the ears close in and to make the head round and shapely. Babies became so comfortable in their boards that they would not sleep unless they were laced inside. When a baby outgrew the board, he or she kept it around because it provided a feeling of security. It was in this way that the young were prepared to contribute and function as worthy members of the Sin-Aikst.

The preparation of the Sin-Aikst young began at an early age. At the ages of six and seven, boys and girls were required to search for spirits that would help and protect them throughout their lives. To do this, they were sent on short excursions away from their dwellings. Sometimes, the destination would be by a creek, at a bench overlooking the Columbia River, or on the crest of a nearby hillside. They were required to return with a container of water or some object as proof that they had actually reached their destinations and spent time there. Grandparents or elders of the tribe closely monitored the children.

Serious teaching began at this time. The children received instruction on the legends of the tribe and family history. Tribal ways and tribal laws were also taught. If there were no grandparents or elders in the family, a tribal elder was brought in to teach the child.

When children were eight and nine, more strenuous training began. The day started with a cold bath in the morning in a stream or river. Long runs in the forest and the mountains built strength and endurance, and children also learned how to swim. Boys were taught to make weapons and fishing and hunting gear, and received instruction on how to use them. Girls were taught about the care of the young to prepare them for motherhood in the future. They also learned how to maintain their dwellings and prepare meals. The girls were shown where and how to gather roots, herbs, and other important plants. They observed and began to understand the process of tanning deer hides into buckskin to serve a variety of uses.

As the children grew older, they were sent farther away to search for guardian spirits and other spirits that would help them in life. They took with them some article like a piece of fur, a feather, or an animal bone and were told to leave the article at the place of destination. Each child was expected to spend the night alone in hopes of making contact with the spirits.

Guardian spirits were found in a variety of places. Contact could be made at any time. The spirit could appear in water, in the forest, on a mountaintop, in animal carcasses, or at a sweat lodge. Exceptionally powerful spirits came from thunder and lightning. Spirits sometimes came to a child in a vision or a dream. Some took the forms of animals or other natural objects like trees. The spirit would sing its spiritual song for the child to memorize, and from then on, the spirit would come to the aid of the seeker when the song was sung. Once contact was made, the spirit became a power to that person for life.

It was important that the child acquire more than one spirit because other powers came with other spirits. A child with only one spirit might have a harder time resisting a person with more or stronger spirits. A number of spirits provided greater future success in life for the bearer. The practice of searching for spirits continued until puberty, when strenuous work was added to the learning routine to teach the young responsibility.

Parents always impressed on their children the importance of obedience to their elders. While power and guidance for life came from a spirit, it was the elders, experienced in tribal traditions, who explained the fine points in the usage of power. They established the social context for the approved practice of using those powers within the tribe. They also emphasized the value of the family. Without family backing, it was difficult to become a person of consequence within the tribe. Children were taught how to bring honor to the family and to live in ways that gained respect from others.

Religion was not an isolated part of life for the tribe. It was deeply ingrained in the lives of the People, who practiced it and abided by it daily. The primary importance of religion was for harnessing power. The forces of nature and all beings, from the mystery of lightning and thunder to the beauty of a flowing waterfall, were sought as sources of power that formed the basis of the Sin-Aikst religion.

I thought often about my mother's stories of the early days of the Sin-Aikst. She told me that her father, White Grizzly Bear, believed that there was power everywhere the Sin-Aikst lived. He said the sun had power and could light and warm the day. The moon and stars had power to light the way at night so all could see. White Grizzly Bear said the land was the mother of all things and, if treated with respect, would always provide for us.

My mother went on to say that the water had power and would provide life for the People, all beings of the forest, and the great salmon that came up the river. She said that the eagle that glided with the wind had the strongest power of all birds. She added that all beings of the forest had power, and the powers of the coyote and the salmon were especially strong. My mother said Coyote could do many things with his power. He could transform himself into a man and back again into the Coyote.

My mother told me that Coyote was clever and deceptive and was forever playing tricks on other beings. During difficult times, I often heard my mother remark, "I will overcome these problems with my Su-mich [power]."

My mother said she was born on Red Mountain near Rossland, British Columbia. Her early years were spent across the river from Castlegar where the Kootenay River flows into the Columbia. She told me that the Sin-Aikst had a different way of life from the Lakes Indians of today.

White explorers who first encountered the Sin-Aikst reported that the People were of average height and size. They also stated that the People had hazel-colored eyes. The white explorers observed that the Sin-Aikst were adept at designing and constructing suspended bridges for pedestrian traffic. These bridges spanned narrow and swift-flowing parts of the Columbia River and allowed fishermen to transport salmon and supplies from one side to the other. When the explorers observed the Indians fishing at Kettle Falls, they were impressed with the People's ability to catch salmon. The white explorers were also amazed at the number and sizes of salmon that were caught. They did not know that two tribes of Indians, the Swhy-ayl-puh and the Sin-Aikst, were caretakers of the falls. They could not distinguish between the two tribes in the beginning.

Years later, during the mid-1800s, white people learned that the Sin-Aikst were a distinct tribe made up of the Upper and Lower Sin-Aikst bands. They learned that the tribe's homeland included Kettle Falls and reached about a hundred miles north of what is now Revelstoke, B.C. The white people also learned that the homeland of the Sin-Aikst was always close to the Columbia and Kettle Rivers.

In these early times, the life of the tribe was ruled by the seasons. Spring, with its warmer weather, brought fresh food for the People. The women, elders, and the young busied themselves gathering roots and plants for food and healing and prepared them for storage. Sporadic hunting of small game and fishing for rainbow trout and Dolly Varden in the streams and lakes occurred near and above Kettle Falls. It was a great relief for the People to have fresh food after the long cold winter.

The People left their winter encampments in wind-sheltered valleys—east and west of the river, near Marcus, Bossburg, and Northport—when the weather grew warmer. They moved close to the Columbia River, where they spent most of the summer months. Roots were a staple in the People's diet, and small bands began gathering a variety of roots in the hills at this time. Once gathered, the roots were cleaned, processed, and dried for future use. In the lowlands, a large variety of plants were gathered and prepared for food, medicine, and many other uses.

The great harvest of salmon began in June, when mature salmon returned from the shores of Alaska and began their 704-mile journey from the mouth of the Columbia to Kettle Falls. The bands moved to the banks of the river and caught the salmon that were not strong enough to clear the falls. This method of fishing ensured that only the strongest fish went on to spawn. The tremendous harvest lasted until late summer. The People dried and smoked the salmon and stored the fish away in large quantities. Later, after the young salmon hatched and reached a certain size, they prepared to make their long journey down the Columbia, into the Pacific Ocean, and north to Alaska as their forebears had done before them.

In August, women, children, and the elders traveled to the mountains to harvest huckleberries. Many were stored in special baskets to keep them fresh for eating, and others were dried for future use.

Over the centuries, the Sin-Aikst gained extensive knowledge of the environment and its produce. It was commonly known which roots, plants, and berries were important for food, medicine, and other uses. To serve their needs, the bands had to know where these plants grew in abundance.

The camas root was a principal staple. The white camas root was found in the Davenport area, and the black camas root was harvested around Kettle Falls. Bitterroot was very nutritious and healthful; it was also used as a staple, boiled and eaten by itself or with serviceberries. The bitterroot was found along the Okanogan River and in parts of the country near Owhi Lake, close to Nespelem. Black moss, another staple, was abundant. The People combined it with various leaves, barbecued it, and enjoyed it as a dessert.

Huckleberries were plentiful and a favorite of the People. The berries were eaten fresh during the harvest season in August, and large amounts were also sun-dried and stored for future use. Huckleberries grew on Red Mountain near Rossland, B.C., and bands of both Upper and Lower Sin-Aikst traveled from afar every August for the harvest. The mountain was a favorite gathering place for the bands of Sin-Aikst people. They met and recounted their lives and adventures, and the young formed close relationships that led to long-lasting friendships or marriages.

Foam berries were picked and dried, then cooked. Sometimes they were whipped into a foamlike consistency that resembled whipped cream. Gooseberries were found along the river. Hazelnuts were eaten right away and also stored for future use. Wild carrots seasoned venison, rabbit, or bear soup. Peppermint was a favorite plant for making tea.

The Sin-Aikst used various plants and berries for other purposes, too. The bark of the willow tree produced a purple dye that was used to color buckskin, and a dye made from canary yellow moss, gathered from pine trees, gave its hue to buckskin, cornhusk bags, horsehair, and porcupine quills. Tule fluff made up the disposable part of a baby's buckskin diaper. The Sin-Aikst split red willow into thin planks and carved the planks into serving vessels because the red willow complemented the taste of cooked fish or meat. Pitch from pine tree bark was used as chewing gum by youngsters.

Cassara buckthorn bark was used as a laxative, and tea brewed from choke cherries offered a remedy for dysentery. Severe infections were treated with a mixture of crushed elderberry leaves and nettle leaves. Marijuana was used as an anesthetic and was also commonly smoked by the elders. Balsam tea was used sparingly to cure coughs and other throat ailments. Tea made from the bark of the red willow relieved the irritation of eye infections.

Sometimes, excessive sharing of food with friends and visitors reduced supplies to the extent that the remainder had to be rationed. Fishing through the ice and hunting small game helped the People sustain themselves until the weather warmed with the coming of spring, and the cycle began anew.

During late fall, hunters went out alone or in teams to hunt deer, elk, moose, bear, and caribou in the mountains. This was the best time to hunt large game.

When the horse became a part of the tribe in the mid-eighteenth century, the more adventurous hunters and warriors were able to travel longer distances. The tribe became nomadic, and tepees replaced the pit houses and lodges used in the earlier permanent villages. These new shelters, made of buffalo and elk hides, were light and easy to transport. Hunters were now mobile and could reach the Great Plains with ease to hunt the buffalo. Hunting parties might be gone for two months or more.

After the buffalo were killed, the hides were removed, dried, and wrapped for transport home. They were later processed and tanned to make clothing, footwear, containers, and shelters. The meat was smoked and dried.

It became a practice during this time to ride east to raid the Blackfeet and steal their horses. This was a risky business because the Blackfeet were dangerous and relentless warriors. Sometimes, the more daring members of a raiding party did not return. Often, the Sin-Aikst were ambushed by the Blackfeet, and fierce battles ensued. Warriors on both sides were wounded or killed during these encounters. The Blackfeet would retaliate and travel west to kidnap Swhy-ayl-puh and Sin-Aikst women. Many of the women were fair, attractive, and desirable to the Blackfeet.

Over the years, the Upper Sin-Aikst developed a unique way of hunting deer. They trained dogs to drive the deer from the hills and mountains to the banks of the Columbia River. Hunters waited in canoes until the deer were within range. When they were close enough, the hunters used their bows and arrows. Other game, like caribou, were hunted as the herds passed through the Sin-Aikst country near Nakusp. Mountain sheep and mountain goat were pursued at higher elevations as hunters combed the mountains.

After the kills, the game was skinned. Meat was cut with the grain into long strips and dried and smoked for future use. Hides were processed and tanned for making clothing, gloves, and footwear. Horns became tools or utensils. Hardly any part of the large game animal was left unused.

The terrain around the Arrow Lakes was steep. Mountains and thick forests ended abruptly at the banks of the Columbia River. Horses could not maneuver easily in that type of country and could not be used effectively for traveling or hunting by the Upper Sin-Aikst.

For this reason, the Upper Sin-Aikst fabricated a special canoe to transport them to wherever they wished to go. This canoe was made from a single slab of bark from the white pine tree. It was formed and secured with thong and resin over a framework of cedar strips. The length of the canoe was usually between fifteen and seventeen feet, and the ends of the canoe slanted downward toward the water and formed a point. The canoe had a simple but beautiful form. It looked fragile but proved flexible and rugged in use. The canoe sat low in the water, and when it was paddled, it glided easily and was not greatly affected by the wind; instead it rode securely and gracefully in the water. The canoe was an important vehicle for hunting and transportation.

Over time, however, horses became important to the Lower Sin-Aikst. Extended areas of flat terrain made it suitable to hunt large game like deer, elk, and moose from horseback. The large game animals were not afraid of horses, and hunters were able to close in and make easy kills. Greater numbers of large game could be hauled away easily with horses and taken back to the distant campsites.

Before the heavy snows fell and the cold set in, the People moved into valleys and areas away from the river that were sheltered from the strong winds. Others sought similar terrain at the Arrow Lakes in what is now British Columbia. They prepared tepees for the cold weather by fastening liners made of tule mats or hides to the interior for insulation. When fires were built in the center of the tepee, the heat remained inside to provide warmth for the occupants.

During the evenings in the tepees, the People told stories. They shared legends of the beings of the forest and the river. Stories of Coyote were told. Coyote was an unusual being, and the legends about him were numerous and always interesting to the Sin-Aikst.

One of the favorite Sin-Aikst stories of Coyote reveals how some of the smaller rivers that flow into the Swah-net-ka (Columbia River) received salmon in the beginning, while others did not. The story tells what influenced Coyote to leave salmon at certain rivers as he traveled north to the Kettle River.

One day, Coyote traveled up the Swah-net-ka with a large number of salmon. It was his intention to leave salmon in the rivers that flowed into the Swha-net-ka. When Coyote reached the Okanogan River, he left most of the salmon at the mouth of the river and traveled up the Okanogan with the rest. He reached the Smil-ka-meen River. He asked for a wife from the tribe there but was repulsed by her. The woman said her tribe did not eat salmon that were old and ready to die. Coyote was insulted, and he chose not to leave any salmon with the Smil-ka-meen people. He built a waterfall above the mouth of the river that prevented the salmon from going upriver.

Coyote continued in search of a wife up the Okanogan River to the outlet of Osoyoos Lake. The Indians there gave him a wife, and in return Coyote allowed salmon to remain and spawn there to this day.

Coyote soon grew tired of his wife and continued up the Okanogan to Penticton. He asked for a wife and was promised one by the people there. In return, Coyote left some salmon. Coyote then traveled to Okanogan Lake. The people there only laughed when Coyote asked for a wife. This angered Coyote, so he returned to Penticton. He discovered that his intended wife had married another man. Coyote was disappointed, so he made Okanogan Falls. He decided to leave the few salmon that were already there to spawn.

Coyote continued up the Swah-net-ka until he reached the mouth of the Sanpoil River. He traveled up the Sanpoil and came to an encampment of people. Coyote asked for a wife, and the people gave him a young maiden. He was pleased and left a great number of fine salmon for the Sanpoil to enjoy.

Coyote soon tired of his Sanpoil wife. He continued his journey, leading a large number of fine salmon up the Swah-net-ka. He reached the mouth of the Spokane River and traveled upriver until he encountered the Kalispel Indians. Coyote asked for a wife, but they laughed at him. They told Coyote that they preferred their camas roots. Coyote was angered, and he built Spokane Falls so that the salmon could not pass up the river.

Coyote returned to the Swah-net-ka. He turned north. Coyote traveled until he reached the Kettle River. He went up the river in search of a new wife. He reached Canyon Gulch near Curlew. Coyote found a village of people. He asked for a wife, but the people laughed at him. They told Coyote that they did not eat salmon that were ready to die from making eggs. The people told Coyote that they ate white fish from the river. Angered, Coyote told them they could continue to eat their white fish. Coyote built the falls at Cascades, B.C. No salmon ever passed beyond those falls.

Coyote came to a beautiful area a few miles south, where the Kettle River joins the Swah-net-ka. He met people he liked, the Sin-Aikst and the Swhy-ayl-puh. He decided to build a great waterfall (Kettle Falls) after they gave him a handsome maiden for a wife. Coyote left a large number of very fine salmon. He told his new friends that many tribes would come to ask or trade for salmon in the future. They would bring many types of food to trade for the salmon.

Soon, Coyote left to search for new adventures. This was his way. The salmon continued to come to Kettle Falls in great numbers every year. Many were caught for food by the tribes, and the rest struggled to clear the falls to go upriver to spawn and complete their circle of life.

Once winter set in, the women busied themselves making clothing, robes, and other articles such as headgear. Buckskin was the material used for most of the clothing, and sometimes rabbit skin was added as adornment to increase the comfort of the attire. The Upper Sin-Aikst Indians used little ornate trim on their clothing, but the Lower Sin-Aikst were attracted to decoration and used it. Headgear of the Upper Sin-Aikst was made from birch and cedar, while the Lower Sin-Aikst used skins and fur. Meanwhile, the men built and repaired hunting, trapping, and fishing gear. Sometimes they also designed and made weapons to prepare for future battles.

A variety of coiled baskets of cedar or spruce roots were also made during the winter months or when free time allowed. Many were beautifully designed with intricate geometric patterns woven in. They are now considered works of art. Baskets were also made of birch bark, some designed with flat sides so they could be used to harvest and collect huckleberries. A buckskin strap was attached to allow the user to hang the basket from the neck, leaving both hands free for picking berries. In addition to baskets, woven storage bags of various sizes were fashioned from Indian hemp twine and inner cedar bark, and flat handbags were woven out of Indian hemp twine.

Although the Sin-Aikst Indians did not have to travel great distances to find food, they made trips north and south along the Columbia River to spend time with friends and relatives in different bands. They also visited the Swhy-ayl-puh bands along the river and in the Colville Valley. At other times, they traveled west to visit tribes of the Okanogan and Shuswap and east to visit the Kootenays. The bands shared important information in this way. Continuous year-round travel was an important part of their lifestyle.

One year, conflict arose between the Sin-Aikst and the Kootenays, who both had an interest in the salmon that came up the Columbia where it joins the Kootenay River. Fighting resulted when the two tribes tried to establish fishing rights in the area. The Sin-Aikst finally won. From that time, they controlled the fishing where the rivers join, and the Kootenays had to be content with the salmon that reached the upper parts of the Kootenay River.

Aside from the tepees mentioned earlier, the Sin-Aikst made other structures suited to different situations and purposes. Pit houses and lodges were circular in shape at the base. Most were set about six or seven feet into the ground. The roofs were pitched, supported by frameworks of bark-covered lodge poles, and a single hole at the center allowed smoke to escape. Ground was cleared away to allow entry through an opening in the side. Sometimes entry was through the smoke hole.

The Upper Sin-Aikst covered the floors of their pit houses and lodges with evergreen boughs, while the Lower Sin-Aikst covered theirs with tule mats. Sometimes, tule mats covered most of the lodge. This worked well during the summer months, since the heat and dry air drew the tule reeds apart, allowing fresh air to enter and cool the interior of the lodge. The raised floor of the lodge also allowed the free flow of air beneath to cool the space above.

Sweat lodges were always used by the Sin-Aikst and were located near streams or lakes. They were simple in design and construction, composed of bent willow branches forming a conical framework with hides and bark placed over it to contain the steam. They were usually six or seven feet in diameter. A hole about fourteen inches deep at the center of the house was filled with rocks that had been heated in a fire outside the lodge. With a branch of cedar, bathers sprinkled water over the rocks to create steam, then soaked in the steam while lying naked on evergreen boughs. Minutes later, the bathers left the lodge and drenched themselves in cold water nearby. This cooled the skin and tightened the pores. Sweat baths were used not only for cleansing but for purifying the body before big hunts. Ceremonies like marriages, or special events of recognition accorded an individual from the tribe, were also preceded by sweat baths. The sweat lodge was a quiet enclosure, ideal for meditation and communication with the spirits. Certain protocols were observed during the spiritual quest. Often this was done in privacy and the secrets were never shared. The sweat bath was also used to help fight off illnesses. The body always felt refreshed afterward.

It was into this world that See-Whel-Ken was born. He is the earliest ancestor my family remembers. He was born sometime before 1800, because in the early 1800s, he became chief of the Sin-Aikst bands in the Kettle Falls area.

During See-Whel-Ken's time, life was good for the Sin-Aikst. There was always enough food for all the bands. Hunting, fishing, and the gathering of roots, plants, and berries satisfied their needs. The People were healthy, and the tribe was strong. The men were dependable providers and warriors, and the women, children, and elders were experts at their chores.

See-Whel-Ken led his hunters several times on journeys to the Great Plains. It was an exhilarating but dangerous experience for all. Younger men who would become warriors one day anticipated their turn to journey to the Great Plains. They would have the chance to test their courage in battle against the Blackfeet and their hunting skills with the buffalo.

This traditional lifestyle continued with little change for See-Whel-Ken, his family, and the People until the coming of the white settlers. The first settlers were French Canadian trappers who entered the Sin-Aikst homeland before 1800. During 1825, the Hudson's Bay Company was established to handle the fur trade near Kettle Falls. The U.S. Army soon followed, settling east of Kettle Falls and establishing Fort Colville to protect the interests of the white settlers who now occupied parts of the region.

See-Whel-Ken could see the importance of maintaining friendly relations with the U.S. Army. He knew that initial conflict with the army would foster a long, drawn-out war that could only hurt the People. See-Whel-Ken had a strong influence on his people. He encouraged his men to hunt and trap for the post at Fort Colville so that the white settlers would not fear his people. During his time, he was trusted and respected by the white people.

When See-Whel-Ken died in 1840, both races mourned him deeply. The memory of his generosity, kindness, and good deeds lived on among both the white settlers and the Sin-Aikst for many years. At the time of his crossover into the spirit world, See-Whel-Ken was prepared in the tradition of the Sin-Aikst. The body was placed with the knees doubled back toward the chest. The hip sockets were broken, and the arms were arranged between the shins and thighs. The feet were doubled back. In this position, the body was bound with thongs, sewn into a robe, and wrapped in buckskin and fur robes. The bound body was placed on a scaffold high in the trees for ten days while the family took turns watching to make sure the person did not revive. When there were no signs of life, the body was taken down and buried in a seated position.

After the burial, a funeral feast was held for all in the band. Friends and those in other bands of the Sin-Aikst and the Swhy-ayl-puh who had been close to See-Whel-Ken were invited to attend. Shamans in charge took See-Whel-Ken's belongings and gave them to certain members present. This was according to the Sin-Aikst tradition.

When a year had passed, the band held another memorial feast to pay its respects to See-Whel-Ken and honor him. Fine gifts accumulated over the past year were given to many who had been close to him. This was a final farewell to the chief of the Sin-Aikst band at Kettle Falls. The memorial farewell is still practiced today by a few Lakes Indians who remember the traditions and ways of the Sin-Aikst.

After See-Whel-Ken died, the great days of the Sin-Aikst ended. Since See-Whel-Ken left no sons, Kin-Ka-Nawha, his nephew, was elected chief. Times became very hard for the Sin-Aikst during Kin-Ka-Nawha's days as chief. The immigration of white settlers increased. Diseases brought by the settlers severely hurt the health of the People. The herbs of healing that had always worked with common illnesses did not heal the strange and deadly diseases brought by the white settlers. Many died. The tribe shrank from 3,000 people to fewer than 400. The boundaries of the homeland were altered, due to the claims of white settlers. This affected the hunting of large game. Soon the numbers of salmon reaching Kettle Falls dwindled because of the development of commercial salmon fishing at Astoria, near the mouth of the Columbia River, by white fishermen.

Catholic priests known as Blackrobes appeared in 1837. Places of worship, like St. Paul's Mission near Kettle Falls, were constructed with the help of both the Sin-Aikst and the Swhy-ayl-puh. At these missions, the Blackrobes worked continuously to convert the Sin-Aikst and the Swhy-ayl-puh to the teachings of Christ and the Catholic Church. The new religion was foreign to the traditional beliefs of the two tribes. The introduction of Christianity, disease, and the loss of important food sources eventually diminished the power of the spirits that had been revered for centuries by the Sin-Aikst. When the strength of the spirits was weakened, the culture began to fall apart and traditional ways began to disappear.

It was a disheartening time for the Sin-Aikst. There never seemed to be answers to the problems they were facing. Confused and unable to protect the People, Kin-Ka-Nawha turned to the Blackrobes for help. He became a strong advocate of their religion, hoping that this would help the People. When Kin-Ka-Nawha became very old, the Jesuits advised the tribe that he should resign because of his age. Kin-Ka-Nawha, nearly blind, agreed, and the tribe elected Joseph Cotolegu as chief. Aropaghan and James Bernard became subchiefs.

A short time passed, then white men who were hungry for gold and other valuable minerals arrived. The provincial government in British Columbia and the government of the United States supported the schemes of these white men. Congress passed laws enabling the miners to remove the Indians from their homelands and stake claims to mines.

The Sin-Aikst and the Swhy-ayl-puh became wards of the government, unable to contest the wrongs they had suffered or defend their rights to what was theirs. As wards of the government, the Sin-Aikst and the Swhy-ayl-puh lost all their human rights. The U.S. government set aside land that had no material value to the white man, called the reservation, and the Sin-Aikst became virtual prisoners there along with eleven other tribes.

Because of these deceptive practices, the Sin-Aikst (now the Lakes Indians) no longer have a homeland. White settlers have taken their homeland, which once encompassed parts of British Columbia and Washington State down to Kettle Falls. The People faced new hardships. Barbed wire fences put up across traditional hunting trails by white settlers interfered with the hunting of large game. Commercial fishing at Astoria continued to severely reduce the runs of salmon at Kettle Falls. This disrupted the natural patterns of survival of the People. They were not able to complete their circle of life. Today, a small number of allotments on the Colville Reservation and in the Kelly Hill area is all that belongs to a limited number of Lakes Indians who are descended from the Sin-Aikst.

3 / The Lakes

The Colville Confederated Tribes were established in 1872. President Ulysses S. Grant signed an executive order setting aside land east of the Columbia River to form the Colville Indian Reservation. The Colville Confederated Tribes included the Colvilles, Lakes, Okanogans, Sanpoils, Nespelems, Nez Perce, Wenatchees, Palus, Chelans, Methow, Moses, and Entiat. These tribes were forced to move from their traditional homelands and settle on the newly formed Colville Indian Reservation, even though they had lived for centuries as free and independent people in what is now north central and northeastern Washington State and southeastern British Columbia. The remaining Lower Sin-Aikst Indians who camped at Northport, Marcus, and Kettle Falls became part of the Colville Confederated Tribes. The Upper Sin-Aikst Indians, few in number, remained in British Columbia. Most went to live with other tribes such as the Okanagan and the Shuswap after losing their land to white settlers. Sin-Aikst Indians on both sides of the border continued to travel back and forth between British Columbia and the state of Washington as they always had, searching for the Way they had once known. Shortly before the Colville Confederated Tribes were formed, the name *Sin-Aikst* was discarded because congressmen had difficulty with it. The tribe was officially renamed Lakes by the U.S. government.

The newly established Colville Indian Reservation was located east of the Columbia River. The reservation included the Colville Valley and the area where the town of Colville now stands. This was great farmland, and the soil was rich for planting. White settlers soon realized that the land was too good to be handed over to the Indians. They petitioned Congress, and the government restored the land to the public domain. Three months later, the Colville Indians were moved to the west side of the Columbia River. Little good farmland exists in that area of the reservation. Indians who had established farms in the Colville Valley and made their living on them for decades lost their land and suffered greatly from food shortages from that time on.

From 1879 to 1886, the Columbia (Moses) Reservation, made up of more than 2.5 million acres, was set aside. The reservation extended past the Okanogan River nearly as far west as the Cascade mountains, ended at the Canadian border to the north, and was bounded on the south by Lake Chelan. But white settlers were moving into the area, and they wanted all the land. In 1886, the U.S. government restored the land to the public domain to accommodate their wishes. The tribes that lived there—the Okanogans, Methow, Chelans, and Moses—were moved to the Colville Reservation. They were joined by the Wenatchees, Entiats, Palus, and Nez Perce after these tribes were also forced from their homelands.

Before 1896, gold and minerals were discovered on the northern half of the Colville Reservation, and the U.S. government opened the land to white miners. Indians were forced to vacate land they had lived on from a time beyond memory. White settlers began homesteading on reservation land in 1900. Because of homesteading, the Indians lost the entire northern half of the reservation, 1.5 million acres of land ideal for ranching and hunting and covered with great stands of timber.

The Lakes Indians had no voice in matters that concerned them and were few in number, so they were powerless against the encroachment

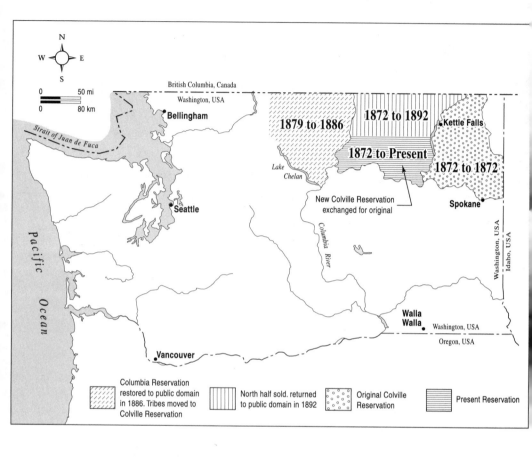

MAP 2. Colville Reservation through history

of white settlers. The other tribes of the Confederation did not fare any better. It became common practice for all Indians to lose land to white settlers. The U.S. government and local law enforcement officials always backed the white settlers, and their desire for mines and farms in the northern half forced the People into the southern half. The Colville Reservation was reduced by more than half, to 1.3 million acres.

Later, when the southern half of the reservation, where the Colvilles and Lakes lived, was opened to mineral entry, miners were allowed to move Indians about and mine wherever they pleased. Homesteading became the law in 1916, and white settlers gained the lands of their choosing. The Indians were left with land that was beautiful in appearance but worthless for farming, ranching, or gardening.

Alex Christian, my mother's father, his brothers Baptiste and St. Peter, and his sister, Marianne, were born across the Columbia River from Castlegar, B.C. Baptiste was born in 1870, and Alex in 1879. There are no recorded dates for the births of St. Peter and Marianne, but they were younger than Baptiste and Alex. Their parents were Christian and Antoinette Christian. The family lived in two cabins located where the Kootenay River joins the Columbia. This area is called Brilliant today. Christian and Antoinette were born at this place as were their parents and ancestors before them. This place by the rivers was important to the Sin-Aikst. Other bands also camped there temporarily. Archaeological evidence reveals that Indians lived in this area for at least 4,500 years.

A beautiful range of forested mountains protects the area, and various species of salmon inhabited the two rivers. From this land base, the Sin-Aikst traveled up the Columbia to meet other bands of their tribe near the upper Arrow Lakes and even farther north, above what is now Revelstoke, B.C. They also traveled down the Columbia to visit related bands that lived and fished at Trail, B.C., and Northport, Bossburg, and Kettle Falls in Washington State. News and events that concerned the tribe were always shared.

Over the years, many of the Sin-Aikst were buried beside the river, and an age-old graveyard exists where the rivers join. Christian and Antoinette are buried there along with their parents and ancestors. Their children Marianne and St. Peter and at least three of their grandchildren—Louis, George, and Julia, the children of Alex Christian—are also buried there.

When the Christian family headquartered near Castlegar, my grandfather Alex Christian hunted, fished, and trapped. He had other cabins beside the Columbia River where he, his wife Teresa, and my mother stayed while he pursued his livelihood. Two cabins were near Castlegar, and another was about five miles north of Trail. Alex had friends in the town of Castlegar and was known by various names such as Christie, Indian Alex, or Alex the Indian.

The white people in Castlegar recognized Alex Christian as an expert hunter. They accompanied him on hunting trips many times during the years he lived there and were fascinated by his knowledge of what they considered wildlife and wilderness.

Alex Christian became very skilled at bear hunting. On one hunting trip, he encountered the white grizzly bear for the first time west of the Selkirk Mountains. Alex was awed by the size and beauty of the bear and believed that here was a being greater than man. He vowed that he would never hunt or try to kill such a great creature. This was in keeping with the reverence the Sin-Aikst Indians felt for the white grizzly bear. When the Sin-Aikst learned of Alex Christian's resolve, they admired and respected it. They decided to bestow the name Pic Ah Kelowna (White Grizzly Bear) on him. He was to be known by this name for the rest of his life.

The Upper Sin-Aikst land in British Columbia is home to the white grizzly bear. This species of bear is unique and is readily identified by its large size and fur that is silver in color. As the bears move about their habitat in the mountains and valleys between Nakusp and the Selkirks, their silver fur reflects the light of the sun and makes them easy to see. The Sin-Aikst had great respect for the white grizzly bear. They felt that the spirit of this large and beautiful bear had great power. The bears' usual habitat is the high valleys of the alpine, but they range at all elevations. White grizzly bears fear no animal or being and can be dangerous when encountered in their favorite feeding areas.

As a hunter, Alex Christian was exceptionally skilled and dependable. He hunted for his family's needs and for members of the tribe who needed meat to sustain them. He was also an expert guide who helped both Indians and whites find their way in that large and beautiful part of the country.

Alex Christian was a quiet man who could sometimes be aloof, but he also became an enterprising man as he tried to survive a changing way of life. The salmon runs had slowed considerably, so he was forced to hunt for large game to feed his family. He moved his family to Red Mountain during August to harvest huckleberries. After picking and storing the berries, he transported them to Rossland, Trail, and Castlegar, where he sold them to white people who lived in those small communities.

Alex Christian was the last in our family to live the traditional ways of our tribe. He traveled from the Arrow Lakes in British Columbia to Kettle Falls in Washington State many times. Sometimes the journey was made on horseback, but often he took the river itself, using a Sin-Aikst canoe.

On one of his trips downriver, Alex met Teresa Bernard, who later became his wife. Teresa was born in Bossburg, Washington, and was the younger sister of James Bernard, who served as subchief and adviser to Aropaghan, the chief of the newly named Lakes Indians.

During his journeys, Alex Christian traveled lightly. He left no trails as he became a part of the environment. He loved the river, the valleys, and the mountains. He appreciated nature and understood and lived with it without causing harm. Everything he saw was alive and had importance and meaning. He did not think of animals as "wildlife" the way white people do. To him, animals were four- and two-legged beings equal and sometimes superior to humans.

Increasing numbers of white immigrants formed small settlements that eventually became populated towns. Trail, Rossland, and Castlegar grew into communities located close to where the Upper Sin-Aikst lived. For a while, the Sin-Aikst and white settlers managed to coexist and carry on peacefully with their own lives, until the number of settlers grew and conflict arose in regard to the land. The white settlers did not want to share what they considered the most valuable land with the Sin-Aikst.

Although the Sin-Aikst who remained in British Columbia were reduced from bands to family groups, they sometimes resisted the white settlers. At times, there was confrontation. In one case, Cultus Jim, a leader of a small group of Upper Sin-Aikst, was shot and killed when he tried to ward off a white settler who had come to claim his land. The Upper Sin-Aikst Indians, few in number, could be manipulated not only by the white settlers but also by the provincial government, which always sided with the settlers. The government passed laws at will to check any attempt by the Sin-Aikst to state their case and defend what was theirs.

In 1912, Doukhobors, members of a religious sect from Russia, arrived in what is now the Brilliant area, hoping to find a better way of life. The Doukhobors settled in the area where the Christian family lived. Within a year, they were occupying and buying land from the provincial government. The Doukhobors wanted the Christian family to move so they could have their land. As days wore on, the pressure became more intense. The Doukhobors had acquired all of the area surrounding the Christian family's land. In August 1913, the Christian family went to Red Mountain for the huckleberry harvest. While they were there, my mother was born. During their absence, the Doukhobors erected a barbed wire fence to mark the boundaries of their land and then plowed

34

their land right up to the fence. The fence enclosed the Christian family's cabins, leaving them no way to approach or exit their land except by water.

The Christian family was angered when they returned to find the fence. They were outraged when they discovered that the graves of their relatives and ancestors had been plowed over. But they were greatly outnumbered by the Doukhobors and could do nothing.

Antoinette Christian and her sons, Baptiste, Alex, and St. Peter, realized that their only recourse was to appeal to the provincial government to classify the land as a reserve. During 1914, Antoinette and Alex sent letters to certain officials in the provincial government requesting that this be done. After much research, a woman who lives in Nelson, B.C., became aware of this and sent me copies of the original letters. I also received additional information, from newspapers and other articles, regarding the Christian family's efforts to save their land. This information confirmed what my mother and other relatives had told me.

Before the invasion of the Doukhobors, the Christian family had been trying to save their land from other white settlers by turning it into a reserve. These efforts began in 1901, when Baptiste and Alex Christian expressed their desire to R. L. T. Galbraith, the Indian agent at Kootenay.

After petitioning again in 1914 to have their land reserved, the Christian family learned that the Doukhobors had already purchased it from John Carmichael Haynes in 1912. Haynes had obtained the land through a crown grant of 198 acres in 1884. The Christian family could not understand how the land they had occupied for generations could be bought from under them without their knowledge or consent.

The provincial government systematically ignored the pleas of the Christian family, and in 1919 the Doukhobors moved in to occupy the land. They had a deed proving they had purchased the land from Mr. Haynes. The Christian family was disoriented. This had been the land base of the Sin-Aikst for centuries and one of their primary fishing areas.

It was also a revered burial ground of their ancestors and of the People. But they had no papers showing title to the land. Small in number, they could not resist the forces that confronted them. They had to find another home. My mother was five years old when the family was forced from their land.

Before they left their home, Teresa Bernard Christian, my mother's mother, died of pneumonia. It was a very sad day for Alex Christian, my mother, and the rest of the Christian family. They placed her in the burial ground, which had been plowed over by the Doukhobors, next to her children, Louis, George, and Julia, who had died when they were very young. Christian, Antoinette, St. Peter, Marianne, and other members of the family rested nearby. Today, the burial ground is unmarked and neglected.

After Teresa died, Alex Christian and my mother, Mary, parted from the rest of the family. They traveled south toward Trail in their canoe. They subsisted on fish and large and small game along the way. Alex Christian took care of my mother. He brought her along on his journeys up and down the Columbia River as they tried to survive away from their homeland. Alex Christian and my mother led a nomadic and lonely life, spending most of the time in a tent pitched along the Columbia. Alex shared much of his knowledge with my mother during that time and taught her how to endure the hardships of his way of life.

Alex Christian knew it would be difficult to raise my mother. He did not have a steady means of income and could not afford to have someone take care of his daughter. His only choice was to live off the land and care for my mother at the same time. My mother found this way of life exciting, and although she missed her mother, she loved her father's care, teaching, and love.

Sometimes, when the sun was setting, they sat on the banks of the Columbia River and talked. Alex and my mother recounted their lives when they had lived in the Castlegar area. They reminisced about Teresa and the other relatives they had left behind. Red Mountain, where my mother was born, was also remembered. This was where the Sin-Aikst bands assembled every August to gather huckleberries and visit. Alex and my mother missed those good days.

Eventually, they journeyed to Kettle Falls to visit with the James Bernard family and other relatives during June when the chinook made their runs. Kettle Falls became their new home. It was a beautiful area and my mother soon grew to love it there. Chief Bernard and Alex talked many times of the problems facing the Lakes Indians. These were problems no one had ever faced before. Both men knew that if solutions were not found, it would be difficult for the Lakes to survive. Deep within themselves, they knew that the Sin-Aikst ways were finished and that the Lakes would have to adjust to new and foreign ways.

Chief Bernard was well versed in the politics of the reservation. He shared his ideas with Alex, who was a quiet man and a good listener. Alex asked questions that were of concern to many of the Lakes. Chief Bernard listened carefully. He knew he would have to deal with these problems and come up with solutions that would be acceptable to the People.

In 1924, Alex Christian and my mother traveled to Omak on the western boundary of the Colville Reservation near the Okanogan River. While visiting friends, Alex became ill. He fought his illness for several weeks before succumbing to tuberculosis. Alex Christian was buried in a simple ceremony at St. Mary's Mission near Omak Lake on the Colville Reservation. My mother was left an orphan at the age of eleven.

Before Alex Christian died, he made arrangements with his friends Charlie and Eliza Hall, who lived in Omak. He offered the Halls half of his 120-acre allotment if they would care for my mother. The allotment of land had been set aside for him and other Lakes Indians by the U.S. government. It was located on the eastern side of the reservation near

Twin Lakes. The Halls accepted the offer from Alex Christian a few days before he died. My mother would live with the Halls until she met and married my father, Julian, at the age of sixteen.

My mother was heartbroken when her father crossed over. She missed his care, attention, and teaching. My mother never forgot their days on and near the Columbia River. She always remembered the happy times at Kettle Falls.

After her father's death, my mother traveled with her foster parents, the Halls, to Kelly Hill, near the Columbia River. They visited often with Chief James Bernard, her uncle, who lived nearby.

James Bernard had about five years of education. That was considered a lot for an Indian. He could read and write and was highly intelligent. This earned him the goodwill of the Confederated Tribes. He was also appointed the police chief of his district in the Kelly Hill area and was nicknamed Captain Bernard.

Because of his position and literacy, tribal members believed Chief Bernard was qualified to transact legal business between the tribes and the government. They depended on his wisdom. People did not know how to hire a lawyer. Even if they had done so, the federal laws of 1887 prohibited them from employing a lawyer on their own behalf without the consent of the Indian agent. Everyone was at the mercy of the Bureau of Indian Affairs because the courts had decided that Indians were wards of the government.

James Bernard was not trained in law, but he followed his instincts. He learned early not to trust white people. The People had been deceived many times by both the white settlers and the U.S. government. Bernard warned the People never to sign any documents presented by the white people. He told them that whites should not be allowed to purchase or settle on tribal land. He had seen firsthand what could happen when the People did not remain vigilant.

In early spring of 1900, surveyors arrived at the town of Marcus under the leadership of a person named Clair Hunt. The Lakes Indians were there to meet and stop them. The surveyors wanted to tape off sections of land to be allotted to individual Indians. After this was done, the whites would take the unallotted land and open it up to homesteading.

Bernard could see the danger in this ploy and went to Aropaghan, who was the chief at the time. Bernard urged him to go to Marcus and forbid the surveyors from entering the reservation. Aropaghan, with some reluctance, finally agreed. Several half-breeds met him. They invited him to a hotel and fed him a big dinner. After Aropaghan had eaten, the half-breeds took him to a store and bought him new clothes and underwear.

In this way, they persuaded the chief to allow the surveyors onto the reservation to section off land for allotments. Aropaghan also promised the half-breeds that they could have allotments like full-bloods if they would buy him food and clothes for as long as he lived. Aropaghan placed his thumbprint on the document, giving his consent. The half-breeds never lived up to their promises, and Aropaghan died a fool and a pauper. Sectioning off the reservation land into allotments proved to be detrimental. It opened the door to white people who settled on choice parcels of land originally meant for Indians. This was just another way of reducing the size of the reservation. It was said afterwards that Aropaghan surrendered valuable sections of the reservation for a pair of underwear.

When Aropaghan died, James Bernard became the spokesman and chief of the Lakes Indians. During his lifetime, he looked after the welfare of the People. He traveled to Washington, D.C., at least three times to voice the concerns and needs of the People. In 1890, at the age of twenty, he journeyed to Washington, D.C., to act as interpreter for Chief Smitkin of the Colvilles. He returned in 1900 with Chiefs Lot and Barnaby to negotiate the boundaries of the Colville Reservation. In 1921, he journeyed again to Washington, D.C., as chairman of the delegation representing the Colville Confederated Tribes.

On one of Bernard's trips to Washington, D.C., a Senate committee-man was reported to have said, "You Indians are never satisfied. Before the white man came, you Indians were naked; you had nothing; your dwelling place was under the trees. When you prepared for bed, you crawled behind a log and covered your breechcloth with a piece of bark. You were dying off with starvation. Now you sit there, big and fat; you have a house to live in; you are better off now than you were before. Now go and don't come back."

Bernard asked permission to respond.

BERNARD: "I am an Indian, and I do not speak your language well, but try your best to understand what I have to say. Did I understand you to say that the Indians were naked and slept under leaves and bark?"

CHAIR: "That is exactly what I said."

BERNARD: "Question number two. If it hadn't been for the white man coming in, we would have had no house, and we wouldn't be fat and enjoying all these good things now?"

CHAIR: "Exactly."

BERNARD: "All right, now I'll tell you a few things, and listen closely and try to understand what I have to say. Also, I want these words down for the record. A time may come when I may need them, when I come back to this house again. What I have to say is this: Before the coming of the white man, our resources on this continent, if we could sum it up, had a value we could never put into figures and dollars. Our forests were full of wild game, our valleys covered with tall grass, we had camas, huckleberries and bitterroot, and wildflowers of all kinds. When I walked out under the stars, the air was filled with the perfume of the wildflowers. In those days, the Indians were happy, and they danced day and night, enjoying the wealth created by the almighty spirit for the Indian's use as long as he lived.

"It is for me to say that you white men, when you came here and landed, you came on a little piece of bark, and with a few sticks tied together, and a few of you on it. You found us that day in plenty; you had nothing. You did not bring your wealth with you.

"What you are saying here today is that you are giving the Indian something and he should be satisfied. You are giving us something that was rightfully ours to begin with and is ours today. You white men have never paid the Indians for what you took that day.

"Now I have a tiny allotment, and when I get off this little piece of land, I am up to my neck in muck, and when I drink water from a stream, if I don't keel over dead right there, I come down with some kind of ailment. The rivers are still yellow, but not with gold.

"So this is why I am here today, in search of your promises, false promises you have made to us Indians, and when I complete my work and find the evidence of false promises, then when I am ready, I will come back and appear before the committee."

James Bernard and his wife, Louise, with their two sons, Isaac and John, lived in a small house alongside the Columbia River near Kelly Hill. He was the respected leader of the Lakes Indians until he died in 1935 while en route to Chewelah, Washington, for medical care. Bernard was buried at Pia, high up on Kelly Hill, where his parents, Jacque and Mary, and his sister Sophia are buried. "Pia" means red-tailed hawk in the Lakes language.

Before James Bernard's spirit crossed over to the spirit world, my father, Julian, brought our family to visit him. We were invited to spend the night. I remember waking up in the morning and going outside. A few men were already there, standing and talking. Suddenly, one of them said, "There's a snake under the doorstep." A few of us looked and saw that a large rattlesnake was stretched the width of the door, uncoiled. The man exclaimed, "That is a big snake. Look at the rattles." Another said,

"I'll get it with this pitchfork." He killed it, pulled it out, and stretched it on the ground. He said, "These make good playthings," as he cut the rattles off. He stood and shook the rattles. I thought they made a menacing sound. The man picked up the dead snake and threw it over the hill toward the Columbia River. That was the first time I saw a rattlesnake. I vaguely remembered Chief James Bernard, but I remember the rattlesnake very clearly.

4 / Kettle Falls

My first clear awareness of life occurred while I was walking on a railroad bridge. The bridge crossed the Columbia River to the little town of Marcus, Washington. I was two years old, and the date was July 4, 1933. My mother was carrying Luana, my younger sister. I was walking beside her. Halfway across the bridge, I heard explosions that sounded like gunfire. I asked, "What is that, Mom?" My mother answered, "Don't worry, those are only firecrackers." I asked, "Are they good to eat?" My mother answered, "Firecrackers are not food but playthings of the white people." When I hear them today, I think of something to eat.

After crossing the railroad bridge, we soon reached Marcus. There was much noise as white people celebrated the Fourth of July by setting off an assortment of firecrackers. We stayed awhile and watched the events. Then we returned across the bridge to the Kettle Falls fishing grounds.

The falls were powerful and beautiful. Close in, one was engulfed by the roar of the falls. Here and there, Indians could be seen going in and out of tepees and tents. Horses in large numbers grazed on nearby grassy areas. Several men with spears perched on rocks or pole platforms above the falls. Others equipped with fish-traps made from the limbs of trees waited for the salmon as they tried to clear the falls. Salmon that failed fell back into the traps. Those that cleared the falls went on to their places of origin upriver to spawn. I was awed by their beauty and strength.

For centuries, Kettle Falls had been an important place for Indians of many tribes. Archaeological digs reveal that Indians lived at Kettle Falls more than 10,000 years ago, but many of the elders say their ancestors were there earlier. The confluence of two rivers, the Kettle and the Columbia, with sources far apart, join and create the powerful falls. The banks of the falls were terraced with large, flat rock slabs that reached up to pine-covered hills. Higher elevations produced beautiful ranges of mountains heavily forested with pine, fir, and tamarack.

During June, the salmon arrived in great numbers. Many tribes of Indians came during the harvest season to take their share of this important staple. Tribes came from all directions. Those from as far east as western Montana and the Dakotas came to trade buffalo meat and hides for salmon.

My mother told me that before the salmon harvest, the men hunted deer in the adjoining mountains. They sought not only the meat but the hides to be tanned into buckskin. Since there was no flint in the area, granite was used to scrape the hides. Granite lined the cliffs on the eastern side of the falls. The granite was chipped into the shape of a fan, and the cutting edge was chipped further to create an edge that would remove the hide from the deer.

The hide was considered green as it came off the animal. It was soaked in water, and then weighted down with rocks for two or three days. When the hair was loose, the hide was placed on a smooth post about six feet long and six inches wide and was braced against a tree for support. A deer rib, or later a dull butcher knife, was used to scrape the hair off the hide. People did this by leaning against the end of the post and pushing with both hands in a strong downward motion.

When the hair was off, the hide was washed and hung to dry thoroughly. It was then given its first smoking over a smudge fire of rotten fir wood and underwent another soaking in lukewarm water overnight. The next day, the hide was drained by attaching it to a pole at one end, wrapping the other end around a sapling, and twisting the hide tightly by turning the pole. Next, the hide was worked until dry. It was stretched in a log frame and rubbed with the main stem of a deer's antler that had been shaped for that purpose. It was again soaked overnight in warm water, mixed with crushed brains, and boiled in the whitish liquid. The smell of this activity was unpleasant to me. The first time I saw this process as a boy, I watched in wonder. I stood for a long time studying every move.

After soaking, the hide was stretched, rubbed, and dried. Then the process was finished unless the hide was going to be dyed. If it was meant to be golden brown, it was smoked over a smudge of rotten fir, or over rotten cottonwood, if the desired color was yellow. Smoking the hide made it water-resistant and pliable when dry. Finally, the buckskin was ready for use.

At least eight large bands of the Sin-Aikst Indians lived where Marcus, Bossburg, and Northport now stand. Other bands were situated at Kettle Falls. Bands also existed up to and above Trail, B.C., while some resided on the Kettle River to the west. Dividing the tribe into bands had its advantages. When members were not fishing at Kettle Falls, they hunted for deer, elk, and other large game. It was easier to do this with smaller numbers of hunters. Smaller camps were easier to maintain and clean. The bands were more mobile and moved easily from place to place. Their horses could graze without competing for the wild grass. The principal gathering area for all the Sin-Aikst during the salmon runs was on the western bank of the Columbia. Indians pitched hundreds of tepees and lodges along the shore as they prepared for the harvest.

At times, when visiting the falls, I sat on a hillside and looked at the campsites below. Tepees were positioned everywhere near the river and on the rock ledges that terraced the hillside. Many horses grazed nearby, and wagons were parked near the tepees. Children and dogs played on and under the wagons while women were busy preparing meals over cooking fires. Older children waded or swam in the slow-moving parts of the river, close to shore.

My mother told me that in earlier days Sin-Aikst canoes were seen everywhere. She said the Upper Sin-Aikst journeyed downriver in many canoes. They came from the Arrow Lakes in British Columbia to fish during the chinook runs at Kettle Falls in June. The Upper Sin-Aikst would cut through the swift-moving river in their canoes to reach the western and eastern banks. They went to Hayes Island to pick up salmon and other supplies and return them to land. My mother also said that in the early days, the salmon runs and the fish themselves were much larger.

Men sat cross-legged on the ground in several groups. There was continuous talk in both English and Sin-Aikst. Sometimes there was laughter as Indian jokes and stories were exchanged. There was never-ending activity that always seemed relative to the roar and flow of the falls.

The tepees were beautiful as they rose from the earth, their lodgepoles reaching for the sky. Many had geometric or symbolic designs painted on their sides, which told something about the occupants. The site was colorful and full of life. At night after the sun had set, people built fires inside the tepees. Wisps of white smoke escaped softly past the crossed poles at the tops of the tepees. The red glow of the fires radiated through the sides, so that the tepees resembled lanterns from a distance. The glow of the fires within the tepees was warm and inviting as it penetrated the darkness.

During the salmon harvest, the head authority at the falls was the appointed Salmon Chief. Before any nets or traps were set or fishermen were positioned, he stood near the lower falls, facing downriver, and prayed. The Salmon Chief welcomed the arrival of the chinook. He apologized and thanked those salmon that would be speared or taken in the traps. He assured the chinook that most would be allowed to go upriver to spawn and bring forth their young. The Salmon Chief spoke the traditional greeting to the chinook every year in June when the great runs began.

It was the responsibility of the Salmon Chief to see that the closely related tribes, the Swhy-ayl-puh and the Sin-Aikst, shared equally in all salmon that were caught. Other tribes that came to fish at the falls were also treated fairly by the Salmon Chief, and they were always welcome. According to Sin-Aikst tradition, the first Salmon Chief was chosen by Coyote.

Then Coyote made Beaver the Salmon Chief. "The people of many tribes will come here to fish." Coyote said to Beaver. "You will be chief over all of them. You must share the salmon with everyone who comes. There will always be enough for everyone. You must never be greedy and you must see to it that no one else is greedy."

The Indians used simple but successful methods of catching salmon. Sometimes they made baskets and hung them from a pole that extended over the falls. When salmon failed to clear the falls, they fell into the basket. Spears were an effective but dangerous method of fishing. I remember that the fishermen had to balance on a simple narrow platform consisting of two poles tied together. The poles were anchored in the rocks and suspended over the falls. Salmon were speared as they struggled to clear the falls. They were heavy and strong and fought vigorously. The spear point was secured to the shaft with strong cord and was designed to disconnect from the shaft when it entered a salmon. The fishermen were then able to pull in the fish using the cord, which involved less risk. It was not uncommon for salmon to weigh 100 pounds in those days. Fishermen often lost their balance while they were struggling with the salmon and fell into the churning water. Some did not survive the day.

While some men fished, others cleaned the salmon and placed them on wooden racks for smoking and drying. Fires for preparing the fish threw heat and smoke upward. I remember the distinct smell of this activity wafting throughout the area. The men fished, and the women remained at the campsites and prepared meals. Children and their dogs were everywhere, playing on the rock ledges or in the shallow parts of the river.

There was a constant movement of Indians and horses. Indians arrived and departed throughout the day on horseback and in horse-drawn wagons. Dried salmon, personal belongings, and fishing equipment were loaded into wagons in preparation for the trip home. When they left, other Indians moved in to occupy the vacated space.

Greater numbers of Indians gathered at the falls during the month of June, and the harvesting of salmon continued until October. Different tribes habitually camped on certain sides of the river while they were at Kettle Falls. The east side of the river was usually taken by the Kalispel, Spokane, Coeur d'Alene, and Flathead Indians. On the west side of the river, the Okanogan, Nespelem, Sanpoil, and Wenatchee made their camps. The Colville and Sin-Aikst occupied both sides of the river and oversaw the fishing.

When the Indians were through fishing for the day and preparations for drying the salmon were complete, various activities took place. Athletic contests such as foot racing, horse racing, wrestling, and swimming races were held. Tribes competed with other tribes, and onlookers bet on contestants with excitement and anticipation. At night, stick games and gambling took place. Tribes that regarded drumming and singing as important performed for the appreciation of all. Trading was also a significant activity and involved both functional and decorative goods.

Salmon was a central part of the Indian diet. Dried and smoked, it kept for several months and was served with roots, plants, and berries.

This was the menu for most meals. Wind-dried salmon was favored and could be stored for even longer periods of time.

Before the mid-1800s, commercial fishing at Astoria, at the mouth of the Columbia, reduced the numbers of salmon that reached Kettle Falls. This began to affect the lifestyle of the tribes that fished at the falls. They had to find other methods of providing food for the People.

Some began to farm and raise cattle. Many planted gardens. The People hunted more for deer in the mountains. Some found work on the farms of white people or with the Hudson's Bay Company. This was a new way of survival for the Colvilles and Lakes. Many had difficulty adjusting to the practice of living in one area and farming. Centuries of experience with a nomadic lifestyle could not be erased easily.

One day, the salmon runs at Kettle Falls ceased. The completion of Grand Coulee Dam, begun in 1933, eventually ended the migration of all salmon to the upper Columbia. After the concrete was poured into the steel framework to form the base of the dam, the great salmon runs ended. The salmon could not clear the coulee, and they were bewildered by the mass of solid concrete before them. Free passage up the Columbia was bred into their being. The instinct was so strong that they tried to penetrate the solid concrete mass that stood between them and their spawning grounds upriver.

This ended the way of life of the Colville and Lakes (formerly the Swhy-ayl-puh and Sin-Aikst) Indians. It brought to a close a great tradition that had existed for centuries. From that day on, life was very difficult for the Colville and Lakes Indians. There was always a shortage of food. The bands dispersed, and the People tried to survive in the mountains, either as families or sometimes alone as individuals. The great days of the Sin-Aikst were over. Age-old traditions very dear to the People became nothing but memories.

When construction of Grand Coulee Dam began, a celebration was held at the site. A large crowd of white people assembled, anticipating

49

a new era. For them, the sad days of hardship, hunger, and the Great Depression would soon fade into the grim past. A few leaders of the Colville Confederated Tribes were invited, a token invitation extended by the whites. The "Chiefs," resplendent in their warbonnets and beaded buckskins, blessed the event with their eagle-feather fans but stood in ignorance of what was really happening. They did not know that it was the beginning of the end for the tribes represented there. From that day on, the tribes descended into an unimaginable poverty.

5 / Inchelium

After the bands dispersed from their traditional areas, our family spent time in areas north and south of Kettle Falls. We and many others tried to live the Way of the People and carry on our traditions, but it was becoming impossible to do. The salmon runs were all but finished, and we were gradually losing the knowledge of roots, plants, and herbs. Only the elder women seemed to know how and where to find them. I saw the women at times, out in the fields digging or bringing in bundles of plants from the hills.

The elders told us that the land we were forced to live on now was not as good as our original homeland. They said that Kettle Falls and the land in British Columbia up to Revelstoke was the best land. They said the roots and herbs were more abundant and of higher quality there.

Because of food shortages, the People were dependent on commodities, or food provided by the U.S. government. The traditional practice of fishing and gathering had changed. Over time, only the stories shared at night by the elders helped us remember the good times enjoyed by those who had passed before us.

Every year, our family went to visit those who had crossed over to the spirit world and were buried at Pia. On Memorial Day, the People assembled to pay their respects to friends and relatives at Pia. James

Bernard and his friends built the small Catholic church, which still provides a place of worship for those who are Catholic.

About forty miles south of Pia, several Colvilles and Lakes banded together to form a small community. The community grew into a town, and because of its location it was called Inchelium. The small town derived its name, which means "where small waters meet the big water," from its location between Hall Creek and Stranger Creek. Specifically, it is located where Hall Creek and Stranger Creek flow into the Columbia River. The People settled there to escape the avarice and injustice of the white people who had taken their land in the Colville Valley and the northern half of the original Colville Reservation. This land is the beautiful area of a million and a half acres directly north of the Colville Reservation. Eventually, more of the People moved to Inchelium, including our family.

Twin Lakes is about thirteen miles west of Inchelium. The area is mountainous, with an elevation of 3,000 feet. At Twin Lakes, the People could fish for large rainbow, go boating, enjoy swimming, or hunt for deer, rabbit, or grouse. The lakes were a favorite retreat and escape for the People. During the summer, almost the whole town of Inchelium took time off and gathered at North Twin Lake to visit and recount tales of the old days. Food was cooked over campfires, and the aroma spread throughout the campsite and forest. The People slept in tepees or tents during the night. While adults and elders sat and visited beneath the trees near the beach, the young swam, went boating, or fished. Some walked the trails in the nearby mountains and hunted for deer.

At least 350 people attended those gatherings, which sometimes lasted from three to five days. The participants were like a big family as most were related to one another in some way. When the sun went down and darkness came, several people gathered and enjoyed themselves playing the stick games. These games of gambling went on late into the night and early morning.

There was always activity at Twin Lakes. It became a favorite place after the People moved from Kettle Falls. During the winter months, some people chopped through the ice with axes and fished by dropping hooked lines into the holes. They caught many rainbow by this method, adding to their food supplies until the weather became warmer.

Twin Lakes was surrounded by forests and mountains, and four- and two-legged beings abounded. Deer and black bear were always seen, and coyotes howled their songs into the night. If you were alert and quiet, you might even see cougar silently stalking prey. Ospreys fished during the day, diving into the lake and bringing up large rainbow. Bald eagles appeared from time to time to hunt in a similar way. In other areas, red-tailed hawks glided with the wind, searching for rodents or other small game. Horned owls appeared at night as they winged through the trees looking for prey. Squirrels chattered continuously, and the drumming of grouse was heard from time to time.

The lakes were beautiful at night, especially when the moon was full, and it was common to see people rowing boats out on the lake for hours. When the skies were clear, they were always full of stars. Sometimes, shooting stars flashed across the dark skies all night long until morning.

Where North and South Twin Lakes join, Stranger Creek flows east and finally drains into the Columbia. Stranger Creek was a large creek, and beaver continually built and rebuilt dams that formed large ponds. Ducks spent time feeding and resting before flying off to another location. Toward nightfall, fish jumped and took insects that lit on the water's surface.

Tents and tepees were always evident. Sometimes a deer hung from a cross pole mounted in the trees, the result of a successful hunt by the residents. Deer was the meat most people ate because it was readily available. Elk was also a favorite, but it was more difficult to hunt. Grouse, rabbit, and bear rounded out the supply of game.

I always looked forward to the days when our people would gather and spend time at Twin Lakes. It seemed to me that we became a tribe again as I looked at the tepees, tents, and campfires placed among the trees near the lake. The presence of people and horses and the sound of drums at the stick games at night blended beautifully with the forest, the lake, and the millions of stars that shone in the sky above.

About eight miles north of Twin Lakes, Hall Creek flowed from the mountains to empty into the Columbia. The entire length of the creek offered ideal fishing, and mountain trout were abundant. Those who found lake fishing slow and boring preferred fishing the fast water and deep pools created by turbulent falls at Hall Creek.

My dad taught me how to fish when I was five years old. He showed me how to tie a spinner to the fishing line and attach a hook to it. He showed me where and how to secure small lead sinkers. I learned from him how to bait my hook with angleworms and grasshoppers. My dad explained that areas close to the creek, where the soil was moist, were the best places to dig for angleworms. He also taught me to use a flyswatter to stun grasshoppers so that I could grab them for bait. He showed me how to cast my line and pull it slowly through the water to make the spinner turn and flash to attract the fish. I learned how to clean a fish quickly and efficiently, in a matter of minutes. My dad also taught me to identify the markings of mountain, rainbow, and eastern brook trout. Although learning to fish aroused my curiosity and interest, I did not view it as a sport. More than anything, I looked at fishing as another way of providing food for the family.

Sometimes, while we were waiting for the trout to bite, my dad and I sat in the shade of pine trees bordering the small creek. He would fill his pipe with tobacco, light it with a match, sit back against a tree, and talk about his youth as the smoke from his pipe curled upward. He told me he was born in a small village near Manila in the Philippine Islands.

Life was difficult for him in the Philippines, he said. There was no work and little to eat. He told me he was born in 1895 and left the Philippines by boat at the age of seventeen to arrive in the United States in 1912. He said he could speak Spanish and Tagalog, the language of the Philippines. He learned English coming over on the boat and during his years in Seattle and Alaska. He said it was easier to find work in Alaska, where canneries along the coasts hired Filipinos to process and can the salmon as the fishing fleets brought them in.

When my dad talked about the Philippine Islands, I thought he was talking about a land across the Columbia River. At five, I had no concept of great distances or great bodies of water and believed all foreign lands were located somewhere across the river. In the same way, when my dad mentioned being Filipino, this made little impression on me. I thought the Filipino were another band of the People, a band that lived somewhere else alongside the river.

My dad was a talented musician and could play the steel guitar, Spanish guitar, and ukulele. He wrote music and could revise the music written by others to suit his needs. When I was older, I saw sheets of music that he had worked on. During his years in Seattle, he played Spanish guitar in an all-Filipino stringed band. They performed often in the Seattle area before and during the 1920s. Sometimes, smaller ensembles traveled to several ports in Alaska to perform for the Filipinos who worked there.

After leaving Seattle, my dad traveled to Montana and Idaho to work at any job he could find. He spent some time in Spokane, Washington, and met my mother when he visited Inchelium. In 1930, they were married in Spokane, and a year later I was born.

My dad never talked about his early years in the Philippines. He did not reveal anything about his parents. He could have been an orphan. I do not believe he had brothers or sisters. He did say that he had a half sister and once showed me a picture of her.

He loved the reservation and adjusted to the way of life of the People. Everyone regarded him as one of the People. The only time his friends thought of him as Filipino was when they wanted to buy liquor. Since Indians were not allowed to drink or buy liquor in those days, my dad took his Model T across the Columbia River on the ferry and traveled north to the small town of Daisy. He purchased the desired goods with money collected by his friends and returned to Inchelium.

When I turned eight, an older friend brought me to Hall Creek. When I stood in the swift-flowing parts of the creek, I had to hold onto my friend's belt so I would not be washed away. Sometimes the current was so strong it forced my feet out from under me. I continued to fish with my free hand. As a nine year old, I learned to fish Hall Creek without any help. I spent much of my free time experimenting with a variety of lures and spinners. If the fish I caught were small, I returned them to the water. I kept only the larger fish. I knew that the small fish would grow and I might catch them another day.

My dad taught me never to overfish. He said that eight or ten fish would be enough to provide a meal for the family. It was important not to waste food. We all knew it was part of the Way to leave something for others. When I fished Hall Creek in my early years, I never encountered another fisherman or saw traces of another human along the banks of the creek. I came to regard the creek as my private discovery and spent many days fishing and enjoying the beauty of the area. Barnaby Creek, where the fishing was also good, was fifteen miles north and about the same size as Hall Creek. But there were many rattlesnakes along the creek, and walking along the banks required much care and alertness. There were no rattlesnakes in the Hall Creek or Twin Lakes area so it was possible to concentrate only on the adventure of fishing and being a part of the beautiful countryside.

When I tired of fishing, I sat on a hill bordering the creek and watched it flowing by. I sat and thought of many things. I pondered happenings that were puzzling to me. I tried to understand things that were strange and unknown to me.

I also listened to the wind that blew through the trees. When I listened hard enough, it seemed the wind was trying to talk to me. I imagined that a greater wisdom existed within the wind and the trees and all beings that were part of the forest and creek. Eventually, the wind with its sounds and feel became my mentor. Along with the other forces of nature, it became my religion. Much of my reasoning arose from the thoughts, beliefs, and ways of my grandfather, White Grizzly Bear. My mother once told me that her father thought about the powers of nature in a similar manner. She said that the Sin-Aikst were very much influenced by the spirits. They lived their lives in close relationship to the Great Spirit and all the other spirits.

It was during this time that I began to formulate concepts of the Great Spirit. I entertained the idea that it was a force not in the image of man but much greater in power than any other spirit, individual, or people. I felt it would be impossible to see the Great Spirit. I might, at best, sense its presence and know that it was there. I reasoned that the Great Spirit would protect those who lived honestly, treated others well, and tried to be good people.

When I felt I had received the answers to my questions, I gathered the fish I had caught that were hooked to a branch and anchored at the side of the creek. I also gathered my fishing gear and walked the narrow trail home.

Inchelium was the principal center of activity for the People. Houses, sheds, and two stores lined Main Street. There were no sidewalks, and although the roads leading into town were sometimes graveled, the streets in Inchelium were all dirt. When it rained or when the snow was melting, the streets turned to mud. It was difficult to walk through town without spreading mud everywhere. During dry weather, horses, horse-drawn wagons, and cars stirred up dust as they traveled Main Street.

A raised sidewalk made of wooden boards was located at the entrance to the general store. When the weather was pleasant, men and young boys sat there and passed the time, sharing news of interest or retelling stories of the past. Our little frame house was located on Main Street four houses north of the general store. I always enjoyed walking to the general store, going inside, and looking at all the things on display. It seemed that anything a person could want was for sale at the general store.

A large potbellied heater stood in the middle of the store, and there were always people sitting around it on wooden boxes or blocks of wood. They conversed in English or Sin-Aikst. During the cold weather, more people would gather and exchange news around the potbellied heater.

The school building accommodated first through twelfth grades and was located less than a quarter mile south, along the river. A playfield between the town and the school provided a place to play baseball and football. Sometimes, horses were ridden and raced on the field. Beyond the field, the sub-agency of the Colville Tribe was housed in three buildings painted white. There was a small jail cell in one of the buildings, but it was seldom used to retain prisoners. Instead, it accommodated those who needed a place to sleep or others who had drunk too much alcohol during the night.

During this time, Pickles joined our family. Pickles was a bullterrier with short black and white hair. He had a pug nose and large black eyes. His tail was only an inch long, and when he was happy, it wagged quickly from side to side. His short pointed ears were always alert. He was still a pup, half grown, when friends from out of town gave him to us. He became my best friend. When he was fully grown, he weighed about twelve pounds. Pickles became the watchdog for our small house and property.

The town water pump, where everyone got water, was located in the middle of Main Street. In some places, large sheds and small barns were located next to houses. There was no sewage system, and outhouses stood behind houses and stores. The town had no electricity or telephones.

I remember Old Cashmere St. Paul always sitting straight-backed and motionless, somewhere in the shade on Main Street, his gaze focused directly in front of him. If something attracted his attention, only his eyes shifted to observe it. When he talked, his lips showed barely a flutter of movement. When he smiled, only his eyes changed expression and lit up. The rest of his face stayed the same. Tightly woven braids, sometimes bound in dark fur, rested on his breast.

Cashmere was a tall, big-boned man, about eighty years old. His strong, bronze-colored face was a mask of wrinkles. His nose was long and narrow with a high bridge and an aquiline shape. His mouth was wide and thin-lipped above a firm, prominent jaw. He had large strong hands with heavy knuckles, and prominent veins covered their backs. Sometimes, his right index finger moved as he sat, tapping his right knee in rhythm as he quietly hummed an ancient Sin-Aikst war chant.

Occasionally, he pulled a small sack of tobacco from his shirt pocket, took out a packet of cigarette paper from his small vest pocket, and rolled a smoke. He did this easily, usually with one hand, rolling the smoke deftly between thumb and index and middle fingers. When he was done, Cashmere placed the finished smoke between his lips, struck a match on the wooden sidewalk, and lit his smoke. He sat contentedly, smoking and watching everything that happened on Main Street.

Cashmere wore trousers that were sometimes purchased in a store and a homemade shirt with long, buttoned-up sleeves. The collar of his shirt was always buttoned up to the top. Sometimes he wore a beaded buckskin pendant that hung from his neck and was displayed on his breast. He usually wore a buckskin vest. Buckskin moccasins and his high-domed "reservation hat" were also part of his usual attire. An eagle feather fixed in the beaded headband complemented the dome of his hat.

On some days, other elder men joined him. They rode up on horseback, dismounted, and sat with him on the raised wooden sidewalk in front of the general store. Most were dressed much like Cashmere. Those who smoked pulled out small tobacco sacks and cigarette paper to roll their own cigarettes. They conversed in Sin-Aikst, sometimes English, comparing the past with the present. They always favored the times of the past. The men seldom looked at one another. When jokes or humorous stories were exchanged, they laughed quietly. After a while, Cashmere's visitors got up to leave. Slight nods of the head, hardly noticeable, signaled and acknowledged the departures. Cashmere continued to sit on Main Street alone. Throughout the day, other elders sat down to join him, and the talk resumed.

Cashmere enjoyed being in Inchelium and watched in silent interest the events that took place in town. Old Cashmere moved only when the sun shone directly on him and he had to shift his position to place himself in the shade. He disappeared in the evenings. Sometimes he went to the general store to sit by the potbellied heater when the weather was cold, but he always reappeared outside on Main Street the next morning.

Young boys always took time to talk to him and ask for his advice. All of us liked old Cashmere, but we were also in awe of him. We never challenged his place on Main Street. When the weather turned cold, he moved into the general store and sat quietly for hours. With the other elders, he spoke for the most part in Sin-Aikst. His laugh was like a deep inner growl that rose gently from far down inside him. Even then, he looked straight ahead without changing his expression.

He always carried a white flour sack over his shoulder. One day, my cousin Louis, a friend named Freddie, and I were playing on Main Street. I saw Cashmere sitting on the boarded sidewalk with his white flour sack. I asked Louis, "Why does Cashmere always have that sack?" Louis said he didn't know, but Freddie thought there must be something in it. Louis and I looked at Cashmere and his sack, and Louis suggested that we go and ask him.

We walked over to Cashmere, and his eyes lit up when he saw us. Louis asked, "Cashmere, what do you have in the sack?" Cashmere focused on Louis and replied, "I carry my friend." He continued, "My friend is always with me." I asked him who his friend was, and his eyes shifted to me. "I will show you," he said. He opened the sack, reached in, and pulled out a large gun.

Louis, Freddie, and I stepped back, wide-eyed. Louis wanted to know why Cashmere carried such a big gun. Cashmere answered, "In case I see bad people." Freddie asked if there were bad people here, and Cashmere paused before he spoke again. "The people that live here are good, but sometimes outsiders come. They could be bad." I asked Cashmere what kind of gun he had. Cashmere looked at his gun and answered, "This is a .45-caliber Army Colt. It is very powerful." "Would you shoot bad people if they came to town?" Freddie asked. Cashmere's eyes fell on Freddie, and he said, "I would shoot them if I thought they might hurt the People."

We thanked Cashmere for showing us his gun and then walked away. I was glad Cashmere was our friend and a friend to the People. We considered him a great elder warrior. I realized that the white flour sack was his holster, and we came to think of Old Cashmere as the guardian of Main Street. Everyone paid him respect.

From time to time, elder women were seen walking from one place to another. They always wore bandannas wrapped tightly around the top part of their heads with their braids hanging down below. Their dresses were long, exposing little of their ankles, which were covered and laced into high-top moccasins of buckskin. The moccasins were sometimes beaded. Women might also wear wide belts of leather or woven fabric. The belts were adorned with beads or with brass or silver studs. Horsehair woven in intricate geometric patterns provided decoration as well.

The women carried buckskin bags beautifully beaded in floral or geometric designs. When the weather turned cold, they wrapped shawls about their heads and shoulders and held them closed at their breasts.

Some women carried small sacks of tobacco and packets of paper. They rolled their smokes easily and enjoyed them just as much as the men. The women always seemed to converse in the Sin-Aikst language. Sometimes little children accompanied them, with their dogs following along close behind.

The young men and women were beginning to change their style of clothing. Some maintained traditional dress, but others were beginning to mix their dress. It was common to see buckskin vests or jackets worn with store-bought trousers, and shoes or boots were preferred over moccasins. The young men had their hair cut shorter, while the young women curled their hair and began applying makeup to their faces.

Yet it was not uncommon to see greater numbers of saddle horses or team-pulled wagons than cars lining the sides of Main Street. Most of the People could not afford cars so they depended on horses for transportation.

During the winter, Inchelium seemed to drift back to another era. At night, the town looked peaceful as it lay under a blanket of snow with millions of stars overhead. The warm light cast by lamps and lanterns glowing in the windows of houses gave evidence of life in town. Now and then, people could be seen going from one place to another. Some were on horses, and others rode in sleds pulled by horses. The chorus of coyotes in the surrounding hills and lower mountains echoed the occasional barking of dogs. The only continuous sound came from the Columbia River as its powerful currents flowed steadily by.

After the heavy snows, large sleds replaced wagons pulled by teams of horses. I never got tired of watching and listening to those sleds in motion. The soft glide of the sled's runners complemented the silence of the snow. During the Christmas season, small bells were fastened to the harnesses. The jingle of the bells as the horses walked or trotted past reminded everyone that a special season was near.

I remember that after a snowfall, the road that led to the hills provided a great sled run. The run was about two and a half miles long. Horse-drawn sleighs pulled or carried our sleds to the top, and we rode them all the way down to Inchelium at very fast speeds. The large horse-drawn sleighs could handle about eighteen small sleds per trip. The older male members of the family made most of the sleds out of wood. Strips of metal secured to the bottom edge of the runners enabled the sled to glide faster on the snow.

Houses and stores were heated with wood-burning stoves or wood heaters. Supplying the town with firewood was never a problem because Inchelium was surrounded by forests. The Columbia River was still swift and filled with a wide variety of fish including trout, whitefish, perch, and crappie, although the salmon were beginning to decline in number. In the Kettle Falls area farther north, large sturgeon were also caught in fewer numbers.

Here and there, large boulders and rocks on the shore and in the river created an interesting natural landscape. When covered with snow, they had a surreal presence. They provided areas for spending quiet time or a place where young people could play games like hide-and-seek, tag, or follow the leader. The large boulders created pools where people could swim safely and in privacy during the summer, away from the swift-flowing parts of the river.

A ferry at Inchelium crossed the Columbia and landed at Gifford, Washington, which was not part of the reservation. North of Gifford lay the towns of Daisy, Rice, Meyers Falls, and, finally, Colville, which was about thirty-five miles away. People who could afford it and had cars went to Colville to buy food or supplies that were not available in the two small stores at Inchelium. The river was still narrow during this time, and a cable stretched from one shore to the other kept the ferry from drifting too far when crossing the fast-moving Columbia. People also left to earn money during the apple harvests in the Okanogan Valley or to pick hops in the Toppenish area near Yakima. The money they earned helped them survive the rest of the year. However, people could find almost everything they needed in Inchelium. Most were content to spend their entire lives there.

Adults entertained themselves at dances in Inchelium on Saturday nights. Liquor was often brought in and too much drinking occurred, which eventually led to fighting. But injuries and bad feelings were forgotten by the following morning. Sometimes dances were held at Kewa, about nine miles from Inchelium. Covada, about six miles south, and Kelly Hill, to the north, also held dances. While the adults danced, fought, or visited, the young played, ate, or slept in wagons or cars parked nearby. This was always the big social event that ended the week for the entire family. Everyone attended, young, middle-aged, and the elders.

Sometimes people played stick games outside the dance hall. They formed two lines, one line facing the other with a long pole placed in front. The stick game was a form of gambling that the people enjoyed very much. The players on one side hid a marked bone in one of their hands, and the players on the other side had to guess which hand held the bone. While the game was being played, the side with the bones sang songs and beat on the long pole with sticks. At times, members of the audience accompanied the players on small hand drums, to add to the confusion of the other side.

Large amounts of money were sometimes bet, and each bet had to be covered by someone on the other side. Sticks representing collateral were passed back and forth as marked bones were identified correctly. When one side won all the sticks, usually ten, the game was over. Sometimes the game was played without betting, just for the pleasure of winning.

In the summer months, most of us swam and dove off the banks where the creeks entered the Columbia. We also went on long hikes along the river or up into the adjoining hills. Sometimes we discovered small plants with tiny white flowers. These were wild potatoes. We dug them up and ate them as we found them. We also found many wild strawberries in the hills and enjoyed their sweetness while eating them. They were always sweeter than the ones raised in gardens. Chokecherries were abundant, and we ate as many as we could stand, but it wasn't much because of the strong tart taste. Serviceberries resembled huckleberries, but they were not as sweet. We always enjoyed the sour gooseberries that grew along the river. Sunflower stems were also a favorite and were found all over the hillsides during spring.

Riding horses was another favorite pastime. There were always several horses available, since most people owned them for personal transportation. We were used to riding bareback as boys, and the better riders usually ended up racing one another before the day ended. When these riders matured, they competed in races across the Columbia River and back. This was a dangerous contest, and both horse and rider had to be strong to survive the rigorous race. The best riders traveled to distant towns and competed for cash prizes in rodeos.

Another pastime was making stilts from slender lodgepole pine. Blocks secured to the poles provided a place for the user to place his feet. The stilts usually ranged between seven to twelve feet in height. Once a person learned how to balance himself, he could walk forward, backward, or sideways, depending on his skill. Follow the leader was a popular stilt-walking game.

The making of slingshots was continuous. Almost every boy knew how to make them and carried one in his back pocket. We made the thongs out of old inner tubes and used leather from the tongues of old shoes for the pockets. The Y-shaped hand stock was cut from a variety of bushes, usually willow. All who carried slingshots were accurate when shooting them. We spent hours shooting at targets, competing to see who was best.

Other boys experimented with various woods from several trees and bushes to make bows and arrows. Some bows were well made and very powerful, and several boys, especially the older ones, became adept at shooting them. At times, they used them to hunt small game, like grouse, rabbits, or groundhogs.

When the adults could afford it, they pooled their money and sent a rider on horseback to swim the Columbia and travel a few miles north to the small town of Daisy. The rider bought as much beer as he could and brought it back to his friends in a burlap bag. Since Indians were not allowed to drink alcohol in those days, a half-breed who could pass for white was selected to make the run. Depending on how much money had been raised, these drinking bouts could last late into the night.

One night, about three dozen of the People were drinking and having a good time. They were making a little more noise than usual, so the district cop went to investigate. He found that some of the noisemakers were buddies of his. They invited him to join them, but he declined the offer because he was on duty. His buddies insisted that he have at least one beer, and he finally relented. The party became more interesting, and the cop stayed for a few more beers. This continued into the night. The next morning, people passing by the party site could see that all the participants were still there, sleeping soundly, including the cop. People in Inchelium enjoyed talking about this party for a long time around the potbellied heater in the general store.

During the summer, several of the People headed for the Okanogan Valley to work in the apple orchards. Workers were always needed during the apple-thinning season, which offered about five to seven weeks of work. In October, the apple harvest began, and many would go again to the Okanogan Valley to help harvest apples. These seasonal jobs provided important income for the People because there was little work available on the reservation.

In August of every year, almost all of the People went up into the Gold Mountain area to pick huckleberries. Many set up tents and tepees and stayed for a week or more. The huckleberries were a favorite. They were great for dessert and could be dried to keep for a long time. When combined with dried venison and fat, they made a nutritious food that could be taken on long journeys or extended hunting trips in the mountains.

Huckleberry baskets were designed and woven out of cedar roots specifically for the picking and storage of huckleberries. These baskets were functional but were also visually appealing, with their pleasing shape and designs of geometric patterns woven into their sides. After the basket was filled, leaves were placed on top of the berries, and the basket was placed in the shade to keep the berries cool and fresh.

During the evening hours or when the weather was cold, people spent time in the general store. A large potbellied heater was the center of the gathering place, and people pulled up wooden boxes or blocks of wood to sit and visit for hours. Sometimes, the People told stories of Coyote or other traditional stories that they always enjoyed. This was a favorite way of sharing news or past experiences that were of interest to them. Everyone referred to this method of sharing news as the "moccasin telegraph."

The moccasin telegraph was an effective way of spreading news to the entire community. Eventually, everyone in the town of Inchelium took part in the talks at the general store or sat with the listening audience. I enjoyed these talks and meetings of old friends. The jokes and stories about happenings of the past and news of current interest were always pleasant and interesting.

One day, a few of the People saw some white men driving stakes into the benches above the town. They rode their horses closer and asked why the stakes were being positioned. The white men said they were marking the future water levels of the Columbia River. The Indians were surprised to see how high the river was going to rise, and the white men were surprised that the Indians did not know about the dam that was being built. They told the Indians that the new dam was going to be located at Grand Coulee. It would be called the Grand Coulee Dam.

The People were surprised by the news. The dam itself was of interest to them, but when they realized that one end of the dam was to be anchored to the reservation, the news became even more interesting. Later, after they learned more, the People realized that the swift-flowing Columbia would rise and cover the land along the river. It then became clear that Inchelium would be flooded over, which meant everyone in and near Inchelium would have to move to higher ground. This caused great concern.

Discussion took place around the potbellied heater one night. Eaneas, my cousin, asked, "Do you know what's going to happen when the river rises?" Several people answered that it would cover not only Inchelium but all the lowlands bordering the river. Everyone would be flooded out and have to move.

Batiste, another cousin, exclaimed, "If all the land along the river is covered, that means Kettle Falls will be flooded over, too!" Someone else wondered what would happen to the salmon runs if the falls were flooded over, and another person answered, "When the salmon can't get past the dam, there will be no salmon runs. That will be the end of all salmon runs."

At this, there was complete silence in the general store. Finally, Ignace warned, "We cannot live without salmon. It has always been a part of us. Many will go hungry."

No one spoke as we all pondered the coming crisis. Cashmere and other elders were sitting at the back of the store. They listened quietly as one of the younger members explained in Sin-Aikst what was being said. From time to time, the elders nodded their heads and uttered softly "hou" to signify that they understood.

Several in the tribe knew that Cashmere and other elders resented the white settlers very much. Cashmere had said many times that the welfare of the tribe had been greatly injured by the white man over the years. He was also angry that the best land along the river was being lost to the white settlers who were moving in. Cashmere knew the salmon runs at Kettle Falls were severely reduced because of commercial fishing by white fishermen at the mouth of the river near Astoria. He and the elders had also witnessed the devastation of the white settlers' sickness, smallpox, which had claimed the lives of most of the people near Kettle Falls. They had also seen the foreign religion of Christianity misdirect the People spiritually.

One night, another meeting concerning the flooding of the river was held in the general store. Cashmere was heard to say, "We should have fought the Su-Yapi [white men] during See-Whel-Ken's time. We were strong then, and we had many warriors. We could have beaten them. The People did not know that many whites would come to take the land. We did not know that the white man would bring diseases that would almost destroy us."

"There are not many of us now," Cashmere continued, "I think the end is near for our people. I believe the end of the Way is close upon us. Our young will never have the chance to experience and live the Way of our people. The river, the land, and the People will never be the same." Many of the elders nodded and murmured "hou" to Cashmere's grim forecast.

My dad and mother attended these meetings several times. Afterward, they talked about the problems our family would face. One night, after a meeting in the general store, my mother said, "I believe what Cashmere says is true. Things are going to change for us. Living will be very difficult for us here in Inchelium. There is little work now. There will be less in the future." My dad nodded his head in agreement. I could sense some of the problems coming, and I was worried. I sat at the back of the general store and tried to understand all that was being talked about.

At the end of one of these meetings, Florence finally spoke. She talked softly and everyone listened. "We cannot sit by and let this happen. We must try to stop this. The People, both the Lakes and the Colvilles, have suffered much from the greed of the white man. The Colvilles have lost the valley where all the best farmland lies. Both the Colvilles and the Lakes lost much when the white man took our north half. They have taken that beautiful country where the hunting is best. There are great timber stands there, but we have been paid nothing for it.

"This was our land and the trespassers from another country have taken it. We were not given a voice in the matter. We tried to move away from the white man after they took our land. We moved here to escape them and built this town of Inchelium. Now they want to take it away from us. They are a selfish people. They care only for themselves. The state of Washington and the federal government have never dealt with us honestly. The only time they come to us is when they are going to take something more from us."

Sarah stood and asked, "Florence, what can we do? How can we defend what is left?"

After pondering the question, Florence answered, "It will not be easy, but we will have to depend on our council in Nespelem. They will have to send representatives to Washington, D.C. Our case will have to be voiced to the representatives in Congress. They should also try to present our concerns and demands to the President."

Everyone was quiet again as they reflected on Florence's words. She had been a respected spokesperson for the People since James Bernard passed away. Both the Colvilles and the Lakes now relied on her judgment and wisdom in regard to the welfare of the tribes.

Louie finally spoke from the back of the store. "What Florence tells us is true. No one will help us. We must somehow help ourselves. The white man has never cared about our welfare. He has only been interested in our land and things that bring him money. He has always wanted what has been ours. All we have left are the salmon at the falls and this town, Inchelium. When they take that, we will have nothing. It will be the end of the Way. It will be the end of the People."

The talks concerning this grave matter were always orderly. There were no interruptions. Each person's speech was low and measured. The words of each speaker were studied and evaluated. All had respect for the viewpoints of others. There was always concern for each of the People.

Sin-Aikst was spoken so the elders could understand all that was said. Everyone in the general store now saw the gravity of the situation. They could see not only the problem they would soon face but the problems that would plague the generations of the future.

They also envisioned the loss of the power and beauty of Kettle Falls and the Columbia River. The falls and the river were the providers of food and also the source of a way of life. Before the white man polluted it, the waters of the river quenched the thirst of the People. The river was a thing of beauty to soothe the tired eyes of all who were close to it. The cold, moving water of the river massaged tired bodies. It refreshed the People for the coming day. The sounds it shared as it flowed south were like a symphony for everyone to enjoy. All that revered life would disappear with the loss of the falls and the river.

No one could imagine at the time how the People would be able to survive this change. Many agreed that the Tribal Council in Nespelem should travel to Washington, D.C., and voice the People's concern. The U.S. government should come to the People's aid now that they were wards of the government. Those at the talks did not feel anyone had the right to destroy a river or a town where the People lived. They also believed that no one should try to work against nature and stop the migration of the salmon. All agreed that the government must be made to understand that the People would be without food if the salmon runs at Kettle Falls were destroyed. They also believed the salmon had an age-old right to live and spawn their young. This was a part of the Way, and this was how it had always been done.

Of more immediate concern were the homes in Inchelium. Many houses were old and would not withstand a move to another location. The People were poor and could not afford to build new houses. These problems would affect many when the river rose to cover the town. Many were confused and could not understand why the government would do this to the People.

Efforts to voice the rights of the People were ignored by the state of Washington and the federal government. It was as if the People did not exist. No official from the state or federal government came to inform the People of plans or schedules. Compensation for losses was never discussed, and no payment was offered for the construction of Grand Coulee Dam on tribal property. The federal government dismissed all claims made by the Colville Tribe. They considered the matter closed.

6 / Surviving

G rand Coulee was located in the arid plateau country. The weather was usually dry. During the winter, it was very cold, and during the summer, it was very hot. There were no trees, only sagebrush, tumbleweeds, and large rock cliffs bordering the river.

When construction began on Grand Coulee Dam, life in Inchelium became very hard. Everyone had to depend on hunting game for food. Tribes no longer gathered to camp at Kettle Falls, and salmon were unable to reach the falls. Those who did not have enough to eat depended on the generosity of others. There was little to go around, but sharing became a common way of life with the People as they tried to survive from day to day.

The construction of Grand Coulee Dam changed the character of the area. Thousands of construction workers arrived to work on the project. There was heavy equipment everywhere on the project site. Dynamite blasts were heard continually as the site was prepared for the concrete-and-steel base of the dam. A number of Indians were also hired. Most started with menial construction work. Over time, some elevated themselves as they learned the tricks of the construction trade.

Frame buildings along what was known as B Street were quickly constructed above Grand Coulee Dam, and a number of small businesses moved in to cater to the thousands of workers. Taverns, bars, small grocery stores, hardware stores, hotels, dance halls, restaurants, and even houses of prostitution became part of B Street. The street was so busy that it never closed. Construction workers worked in three shifts at the dam site, so there were always other workers spending time and enjoying themselves on B Street.

During late summer of 1935, my dad and mother decided to start a business at Grand Coulee Dam. They put all the money they could get into a small Chinese restaurant. Neither of them could prepare Chinese food except for simple dishes such as pork fried rice, egg foo-yung, and chop suey. The menu was limited, but somehow they managed to keep the restaurant open for business.

One day, a Chinese man came into the restaurant. He looked at the menu and ordered some food. My dad and mother were curious about the man and wondered where he came from. They walked over to him and introduced themselves. The man said his name was Harry Wong. After talking with him, my dad and mother learned that Mr. Wong had come from Spokane and knew how to cook. He was looking for a job cooking Chinese dishes. My dad conferred with my mother. They decided to hire Mr. Wong. The three of them worked closely together. Harry Wong prepared a wonderful menu of traditional and contemporary Chinese dishes. My dad washed the dishes, maintained the premises, and provided all the supplies. My mother waited tables and served as the cashier. From that time on, business was good and steadily improved.

I remember our sleeping quarters—a tent behind the small restaurant. The floor and four-foot-high sidewalls were made of lumber. The top and the rest of the walls were canvas. A cylindrical oil heater about thirty inches high provided heat. A gas lamp gave us light. The tent was located on a sandy lot, and Luana and I spent most of our time playing there.

When we tired of playing in the sand, Luana and I walked the length of B Street and window-shopped. We were the only children in the area. We felt at home with all the construction workers and the people who operated businesses. We recognized several construction workers who frequented our family's restaurant.

Sometimes, when Luana and I walked along B Street, women stopped us and talked to us. They were very friendly, and many of them were very attractive. We saw them often. Their numbers would increase during the evening hours. They were always with different men, and they always greeted us. I remember some of them giving us chewing gum. I thought they looked very nice in their pretty dresses. They wore high-heeled shoes and stockings with seams that ran down the backs of their legs. I remember that they always smelled good, similar to the lilacs and wildflowers that grew on the hillsides near Inchelium.

The thing that impressed me most on B Street was the large number of white people who spent their time there. Compared to the people in Inchelium, they were very loud and boisterous. Inside and outside of taverns, there would be quarrels and fights. Luana and I saw men scuffling several times at night when we walked along B Street.

It did not occur to me then, but we were the only nonwhites living in the area. I did not even think of Harry Wong in racial terms. I did not view him as Chinese until years later. During my first trip to Seattle in 1948, when I was seventeen, I saw many Chinese in the section called Chinatown. That was when I saw that there were other people in the world who were not white or Indian.

During spring of 1937, my dad and mother decided to move back to the reservation. They missed the mountains and the trees. They also missed Twin Lakes. My dad and mother longed for the simple ways of life and the closeness of the People in Inchelium. They sold their interest in the restaurant to Harry, and the restaurant's name was changed to Harry Wong's Noodle Parlour.

From time to time, we went back to visit Harry at the restaurant. When

Harry was not too busy, my dad and mother watched the restaurant. Harry would walk with Luana and me from B Street to downtown Grand Coulee. He bought us each an ice cream cone, and then we walked back up the hill. Harry taught me how to eat with chopsticks during one of our visits. He was a very generous man. Every time we visited him, his first order of business was serving us something special to eat.

People from the reservation traveled to B Street to eat at Harry Wong's Noodle Parlour. Those of the People who worked at the dam would also come. Harry's restaurant became a favorite place for many. Sometimes, when a person could not pay for a meal, Harry provided food anyway and trusted the person to pay him later. Over the years, Harry made many friends in the tribe because of his understanding, patience, and generosity. When he traveled to the reservation to visit, the People greeted him warmly.

Harry had relatives in China and communicated constantly with them through letters, which he wrote in Chinese. Sometimes, his friends and relatives in China sent him special Chinese sweets and fruits. When he received them, he set some aside for Luana and me. He shared them with us when we visited. He explained what they were and where they came from.

One day, while Luana and I were eating a variety of Chinese sweets, Harry gave us some litchi. They had a strange but wonderful taste. The fruit with the sweet mellow flesh became my favorite. As we ate, Harry told us that he came from a city called Canton, a large city in China close to the South China Sea. I had no idea what he was talking about, but I remember him trying to explain where it was.

When business was slow, Harry sometimes took his violin from its case and played simple tunes for Luana and me to enjoy. This seemed to be Harry's favorite pastime, and he always had a big smile on his face as he tapped his foot and played.

In summer 1937, my dad and mother were hired by the tribe to be fireguards in the Gold Mountain area. The job lasted all summer. We lived in a tent off the main road between Bridge Creek and Inchelium. Our tent was located where a road branches off to reach the Gold Mountain lookout. All visitors had to stop their cars at a gate, and my dad told them where they could find places to camp. He also advised on the safe use of campfires to help prevent forest fires.

While my mother and Luana occupied their time attending to the camp area or preparing meals, I tried to catch chipmunks. I designed a trap from a wooden apple box by fastening a heavy rock at the top of one end. The box was tilted, propped up by an eight-inch stick that had an eight-foot string tied to it. I scattered crackers under the tilted box. When chipmunks went under the box to eat the crackers, I pulled the string, and the box fell and trapped them. They were easy to trap, but I could never capture them. When I lifted the box, the chipmunks ran for safety. I continued to play this game with the chipmunks, trying to devise ways of capturing them.

Pickles was always nearby. He watched with interest. He never interfered with my attempts to catch the chipmunks. He was a great watchdog. He was fearless, and he knew that his main job was to watch over the family.

One day, we went to Inchelium to pick up supplies. We were there for a couple of hours visiting friends. When it was time to return to our camp at Gold Mountain, we could not find Pickles. We looked all over Inchelium but could not find him. We worried that he might have gone exploring or that someone might have taken him. When it started to get dark, we finally returned to Gold Mountain without him.

The next day, toward late afternoon, people we knew from the Inchelium area came driving up to our camp. We saw Pickles looking through the side window of the car. When the people opened the car door, Pickles jumped out and ran barking to our tent. He wagged his tail, and we realized that he had hitched a ride home.

Our tent was located near the summit of the mountain, and the nearest drinking water was about a half mile away. It came from a small spring that flowed down a ravine off the main road. When our water supply was low, my dad took Luana and me in the Model T with several containers to get water from the spring. The spring water was very cold and sweet. Luana and I considered it a treat. On some trips, my dad brought my old red wagon, which he had repaired for me. He tied the wagon to the back of the Model T and pulled Luana and me slowly back to our camp. Luana and I always looked forward to those rides.

Sometimes, I walked about the summit, but I never strayed too far. My dad had warned me that bear and cougar were about and it could be dangerous for a boy who was only six and carried no rifle. I was anxious to grow older. My dad promised me that I could have a rifle when I turned eight. He told me he would teach me how to shoot. In the meantime, I carried my slingshot. It was always in my left back pocket, ready for any emergency.

The brisk air at the summit sharpened our appetites. It seemed that I was always hungry. A large log that lay alongside our tent was our table, and I waited with some impatience as my mother and Luana set out the metal plates in preparation for our meals. I remember how good the bacon and coffee smelled as my mother prepared breakfast. It went well with the fresh, brisk air of the Gold Mountain summit.

On September 25, we had to take my mother to the Colville Indian Agency hospital in Nespelem. She was due to give birth to a future member of the family. On September 27, my mother gave birth to a baby boy. She decided to name him Bernard in honor of Chief James Bernard, her uncle. My mother held baby Bernard and massaged his nose gently. As the days went by, I could see that his nose showed signs of a high bridge. He also had dark, piercing eyes. I was pleased that Luana and I now had a little brother.

We returned to our Gold Mountain camp the next day. Baby Bernard

Chief James Bernard at Kelly Hill, c. 1931.

B Street, Grand Coulee, Washington, c. 1937.
Courtesy *Grand Coulee Star*

Kitchen of the restaurant on B Street, Grand Coulee, 1936.
Left to right: Harry Wong, Julian, and Mary.

Mary, Harry Wong, and Julian in the dining area of the restaurant.
Grand Coulee, 1936.

Looking north on Main Street, Old Inchelium, May 1938.
The general store is third from left. Courtesy *The Spokesman-Review*

Main Street in Old Inchelium; if memory serves, it may be Alec Covington
and Pete Noyes at the water pump, c. 1938. Courtesy *The Spokesman-Review*

Bernard and Model T, with Lawney in background,
at Cobb's Creek. Inchelium, 1939.

Bernard holding guitar; second row: Luana at far left, Lawney second
from right, with his arm over Benny Aubertin's shoulder. Manila Creek, 1942.

Chemawa Indian School, 1941. Football field in the foreground.
Brewer Hall, where Lawney had a room, at left. Courtesy
National Archives, Seattle, Washington

Kettle Falls, c. 1931.

Kettle Falls, c. 1933. Courtesy Northwest Museum of Arts and Culture
and Eastern Washington State Historical Society, L94-8.5

Mary Christian and daughter Laura, Tacoma, 1954.

Totem pole dedication, Pioneer Square, Seattle, 1971.
From left: Tom McLoughlin, attorney to H.E.W.; Joyce Reyes, President,
American Indian Women's Service League; Bernie Whitebear, Executive
Director, United Indians of All Tribes Foundation; Bernard ("Buck") Kelly,
Regional Director, H.E.W., Region X. Courtesy *The Seattle Times*

(Above) Bernie Whitebear and Joyce Reyes present gifts from UIATF to Senator Henry Jackson (*far left*) and Mayor Wes Uhlman (*far right*), at the Indian Cultural Center, Discovery Park, Seattle, 1973. Photograph by Bob Miller; courtesy *The Seattle Post-Intelligencer*

(Facing page, top) Lawney working on a buckskin collage, Seattle, 1967.

(Facing page, bottom) Lawney at work as interior designer for Seafirst Corporation, Seattle, 1976. Courtesy *The Seattle Times*

Lawney sculpting Bluejay II in Seattle, c. 1974. Courtesy *The Seattle Times*

The "Gang of Four": Bob Santos, Bernie Whitebear, Larry Gossett, and Roberto Maestas, Seattle, 1997.

Memorial service for Bernie Whitebear, Convention Center, Seattle, July 21, 2000. *From left:* Ed Claplanhoo, Linley Logan, Senator Daniel Inouye, and Father Patrick Twohy. Courtesy John Loftus

(*Above*) Bernie Whitebear, CEO, United Indians All Tribes Foundation, Seattle, 1997. Courtesy Ben Marra, photographer

(*Facing page, top*) Laura speaking at the memorial service for Bernie Whitebear, July 21, 2000. From left behind her are family members Darren, Luana, Lawney, and Kecia. Courtesy John Loftus

(*Facing page, bottom*) A portion of the family at Bernie Whitebear's house in Seattle, Christmas 2000. *Front row:* Adrienne, Recy; *middle row:* Kecia, Laura, Harry, Teresa, Luana; *back row:* Marland, Carol, Lawney

The next generation, Seattle, 2000: (*clockwise from top*) Duran ("Sebb"), Darren, and Recy; Recy, Gaby, Sebb, and Helen; Marland

kept my mother and Luana very busy. Feeding and diaper changes seemed neverending. Sometimes Bernard cried when he wanted attention, but most of the time he laughed in a robust manner as my mother and Luana played with him. Luana also helped my mother bathe Bernard in a large pan in the open air. Bernard enjoyed the baths and always smiled happily while my mother scrubbed him with a washrag and soap. He broke into laughter as she dried him briskly with a large towel.

Pickles was curious when he first saw Bernard. He walked up and smelled him as my mother held him while she was sitting on the ground. Pickles soon accepted Bernard as part of the family, and from then on he was always close to Bernard. He seemed to realize that protecting Bernard was now one of his responsibilities.

A few days before we left Gold Mountain, my mother took Luana, Bernard, and me for a walk along the dirt road leading to the Gold Mountain lookout. Pickles trotted alongside us. Bernard was in a baby buggy, and my mother was pushing him. We were about a quarter of a mile from our camp when we reached a bend in the road. As we came around the bend, we saw a large black bear walking on the road in the same direction, about eighty feet ahead of us.

When Pickles saw the bear, he started snarling and barking. He ran after the bear, and the bear started running down the road with Pickles right behind him. Pickles caught up with the bear and bit him on the hind leg. This made the bear angry, and he turned and started to chase Pickles. We were paralyzed as we saw Pickles running toward us with the bear in close pursuit.

My mother held her ground with Bernard and Luana, but I thought it best to run back to our camp to get my dad. I did not want to leave them, but I was afraid and confused. I ran to our camp as quickly as I could. When I got there, I saw my dad chopping wood for the fire. I told him to hurry. He set aside his ax, grabbed his 32.40, and followed me.

When we got to my mother, she told us that the bear had stopped chasing Pickles about thirty feet from where we stood. Luana said the bear had gone over the bank into the wooded area.

My dad and Pickles walked to the edge of the road and looked down the hillside. He told us that the bear was gone. The four of us walked the narrow dirt road back to camp with Pickles trotting ahead. My mother pushed Bernard in the baby buggy. We were all very much relieved, and the only person who did not seem frightened was my mother. She said there had really been nothing to worry about. My mother said her Sumich (power) was greater than the bear's.

The weather was clear, and we could feel the chill in the air. The leaves were starting to turn color. We stayed at Gold Mountain until mid-October, then we packed our belongings. We took down the tent, cleaned our camping area, loaded up the Model T, and headed to Omak for the apple harvest.

That trip in the fall of 1937 was our last trip to Omak as a family. My dad and mother picked apples until the harvest ended. While they worked, Luana and I took care of Bernard. Pickles was always close by, watching over us. We camped in a tent in the orchard, where we could be close to our dad and mother. Luana and I entertained ourselves by playing nearby. We never went too far from Bernard, and if he cried, we attended to his needs. If we thought he was hungry or needed his diaper changed, one of us went to get our mother. She returned to the tent to feed or clean him.

More than once, young white men drove past our tent and yelled insulting remarks about Indians. Usually, my dad and mother ignored them and continued to work. But this one time, the whites called us "stupid redskins" and "dumb war-hoops." One yelled, "You're so stupid that you don't know a tepee from a tent." Another shouted, "Go back to your reservation. This is white man's country. No dirty Si-wash allowed." They drove away laughing. My mother was deeply offended and angered when the white men called us Si-wash. It was a derogatory and insulting word used by white people to degrade Indians.

Luana and I were puzzled and worried by the behavior of the white men. We wondered why they made fun of us. Our family had never experienced this type of treatment before. I could see that these men did not like us. Luana and I were unsure of how we should react to their insults. We were frightened, but we did not show our fear. The white men harassed us continually during our stay at the orchard. Their actions disrupted our play and made us tentative. We would not wander far from our tent, and we were ever watchful of Bernard.

When the harvest was over in early November, we loaded the Model T and headed back to Inchelium. We drove north to Tonasket and, from there, headed east toward Wauconda. Before reaching Wauconda, we stopped by the side of the road for a rest. Pickles, our bullterrier, was sniffing at something in the middle of the highway.

We saw a car traveling very fast coming toward us up the highway. We tried to call Pickles, but he did not hear us. The car, which was full of whites, did not slow down and purposely ran over our dog. The whites laughed as they drove past, and our family was shocked. I reached down to lift my friend from the highway. As I held him tenderly, blood flowed from his wounds and coated his black and white hair. Pickles had died instantly. I could not believe what had happened. Luana's expression reflected our pain as I carefully laid Pickles on the grass beside the highway.

This incident left me very sad but also very angry. I believe this was the first time in my life that I experienced anger. We buried Pickles by the side of the road. We made a cross of sticks tied with string and pushed it into the soil at the foot of Pickles's grave. I stood beside the grave and prayed quietly. Luana and I could not control our tears. My dad and mother, tending Bernard, who was wrapped tightly in a blanket, were grim and quiet. The sun was setting as we continued our journey home to Inchelium in the Model T. For the first time in my life, I felt the pain of loneliness and despair. We traveled in silence.

As we drove on toward Inchelium, I thought about the incident and could not understand why those white people wanted to hurt Pickles. He had never bothered anyone. All he ever did was watch over our family. I wondered what kind of people those white men were. I decided they were a kind of people I did not like, people to be avoided.

I remembered how the whites at the orchard had treated our family. I wondered why they had behaved in that way. We did not know them and had done nothing to them. These thoughts stayed in my mind as we traveled to Inchelium. It was not good to be traveling without Pickles, and I began to miss him very much. Pickles was my best friend. He had come to my rescue more than once when bullies chased me and tried to start fights with me at Inchelium before I started school. Over the years, I have driven past Pickles's gravesite many times. The sadness and anger come back to me when I think of how he was killed.

Our mother spent much time teaching Luana, Bernard, and me a variety of things about life. Because of her nomadic life with her father, she had never lived in one place long enough to complete school. She was able to attend school for only two years. Alex Christian taught her to read and write. He also taught her numbers as well as he could. He was an expert in the Way of the People and taught her much of the Sin-Aikst culture.

Our mother wanted us to have a better understanding of words and numbers. She knew the importance of learning. Our dad could not help much in this area because he had no schooling. He was a self-made man and had taught himself to read and write, but his knowledge of letters and numbers was limited. He understood the value of hard work and the out-of-doors. He shared everything he knew of those experiences with Luana and me.

It was important to our mother that Luana and I could care for ourselves and keep clean no matter where we lived. We learned very early that it was important to brush our teeth. We understood that we should not eat too much candy or drink too much soda pop. Our mother spent hours reading to us, and by the time I was ready for school, I'd taken the first steps toward learning how to read and write. Luana had the same advantage when she entered school two years later.

My mother talked often about her father, Alex Christian (White Grizzly Bear). She told us of the trips they had taken by canoe down the Columbia River from Castlegar, B.C., to the Kettle Falls area. I had heard these stories many times and felt I knew my grandfather well. I was fascinated by his knowledge of the forests, mountains, and river. Later, I learned to respect his consideration for his family and relatives. These qualities of my grandfather have remained with me and guided me throughout my life.

I used to wish I could have traveled with my grandfather and mother. The country was and still is beautiful, although marred now by buildings and small communities along the Columbia River. The large pine and fir are gone, and only decaying stumps remain. I imagined how very exciting it must have been to see the country during my grandfather's time when grizzly bear, moose, cougar, and elk were around in large numbers.

I remember stories of White Grizzly Bear's hunting adventures. He was a completely confident hunter. Sometimes, he crawled into caves where bears were hibernating. He pulled them out and killed them with his .25-caliber survival rifle. Once, while hunting with a white friend near Castlegar, he killed two large brown bears and a black bear with his .25. He sold the meat and hides to help support his family.

Another time, he found a black bear cub that had lost its mother. White Grizzly Bear took the cub home and raised it until it was fully grown. He kept it as a companion. One day, while he was sitting on the porch in his rocking chair, the bear walked up and playfully hit my grandfather, knocking him and his rocking chair off the porch. My grandfather decided it was time to part company and gave the bear to a carnival that was traveling through the area.

I don't know what my grandfather looked like, although my mother once said that Bernard resembled him. She said they had similar eyes and noses and the same wiry build. There are no photographs of my grandfather, but I did see a picture of my grandmother, Teresa Bernard. She was attractive, and I could understand where my mother, Mary, got her looks.

My mother was a considerate and loving person. If a friend needed help or just someone to talk to, my mother went to visit. She packed a large brown paper sack full of extra clothes and other personal articles and stayed for as long as she was needed. She never used a suitcase if a large brown paper sack was within reach. If my mother knew she was going to be visiting for a long period of time, she packed two large brown paper sacks.

She might talk with her friends about the old days at Kettle Falls. Sometimes they used the Sin-Aikst language to make a point. There was much laughter as they remembered the good times of the past. My mother loved her friends and the People, but she saved most of her love for her children. She was a proud person and faced difficulties in a calm manner. When she was upset, she kept her feelings to herself. She always referred to her Su-mich (power) in dealing with problems.

The year 1938 was to be an eventful year for our family. My dad and mother decided that February would be a good month to move our small house from the town of Inchelium to higher ground because there would still be snow on the ground. We needed snow so that our house could be placed on log skids and pulled to higher ground by a small "cat."

The new site was about four and a half miles away, and my dad and mother selected a lot that was an acre in size. There were several pines and firs on the land and a few tamaracks. The ground was covered with wild grass. A small creek flowed past the property. The creek, I discovered, was filled with mountain trout, and Luana and I were happy about that.

The residents of Inchelium were aware that they would all have to move eventually, before the waters of the Columbia rose and covered the existing townsite. Even the graveyards had to be relocated to higher ground. When that time came, my dad got a job moving graves to selected locations in the new Hall Creek Cemetery. The job lasted for about two and a half months. Eventually, the Catholic church and certain parts of the school were disassembled and transported to new locations in the lower mountains, where they were reassembled by the People.

Grand Coulee Dam was nearing completion, which meant the end not only of Inchelium but also of the lowland areas bordering the river. Those people had to move, too. The new homesites were scattered all over the hills and lower mountains. The town of Inchelium ceased to exist, and many missed the bands and sense of community Inchelium had once provided.

Some of the elders who could not move their houses remained where they were until the river rose and covered the streets of Inchelium. They were determined to live in their homes for as long as they could. I remember wading through water to reach their homes, which were situated on raised areas throughout the town. As the water reached higher levels, the elders were finally forced to move. They lived in tents and flimsy shacks built from whatever boards and materials that could be found.

After our house was settled on our property, repairs had to be made to make it livable. My dad built a shed with steps leading down into a cellarlike space that had been dug out of the ground. The space was designed to keep vegetables and potatoes cool after we brought them in from the garden we were planning to start in the spring. The ground level of the shed was used for general storage. Tools, car parts for the Model T, and some of my mother's extra canning jars were also stored in the shed.

From time to time, we saw other houses being towed to their new homesites. Those who were unable to move their homes transported their belongings by horse-drawn wagon. They moved into the mountains and lived in tents or tepees until they could afford to build cabins or houses with whatever lumber they could find. These were difficult times for the People, and many years went by before they were able to live as they once had in Inchelium.

After the People were settled, our family received visitors who spent time with my dad and mother. They talked and exchanged news for hours. When children our age came to visit, Luana and I showed them our creek and the trout that lived in it. I had shoveled out the pool to make it deeper and wider so that we could wade, sit, or even mud-crawl in it. Our water supply was derived from the creek, and we irrigated our garden with its water during the summer months. At night, we listened to the sounds of the creek flowing by, accompanied by the songs of frogs and crickets. We always passed into sleep to those sounds.

One day, as we worked on our property, friends brought us a small puppy. They knew that Pickles was no longer with us. The puppy had medium brown fur. He made himself at home. We all liked him, and as we played, he reminded us of Pickles. Bernard loved the puppy, and the puppy was especially fond of Bernard. We knew he would be a good addition to the family. We kept him and called him Brownie.

There was always a shortage of jobs, and the only jobs that lasted for any length of time were in logging camps. Several young men worked with the C.C.C. camp clearing trails and building bridges and camping areas in the woods. They also fought forest fires. Those who had good soil on their property planted gardens and raised vegetables to add to their food supplies. During the winter, food was always scarce, and everyone received commodities to help get through the winter.

The commodities consisted of flour, cornmeal, oatmeal, salt, sugar, beans, and macaroni. Powdered milk was also provided. If it had not been for the commodities, most of the People would have had a very difficult time during the winter. When people did have money to spend on food or other supplies, they traveled to Meyer's Falls or Colville to get them. This was not easy because many people did not have cars. They had to use horses for traveling and transporting supplies.

These were not happy times for the People. It was a struggle to survive. When we traveled, we always kept an eye out for game, whether it be deer, rabbits, or grouse. Most people carried a 25.20-caliber lever-action rifle for hunting deer. The shells were smaller and less expensive than the 30.30. Sometimes the .22 long was used because the shells were the least expensive of all.

Mealtimes were not the happy family get-togethers they had been once. We ate whatever was available to replenish our energy, hoping that life might be better the next day. The recreation, play, and sharing we'd known as a band were not to be experienced again. Those great times of living and working together became a thing of the past. Family ties began to fall apart. Relatives were rarely seen and, in some cases, were eventually forgotten.

The year 1938 proved to be the last year our family would be together. We celebrated our last Thanksgiving and Christmas together that year. Our mother's close involvement in guiding and teaching us came to an end.

Luana and I were not aware that there were any problems between our dad and mother. We were at a loss to understand why our mother would no longer be living with us. Our mother and dad had been married for almost ten years, and they seemed to get along well. But we soon learned what the word "divorce" meant and that it was now taking place. We were confused and greatly saddened by what was happening. Bernard was too young to be affected much, and Luana and I tried to keep him busy and happy by playing with him and including him in what we did.

From time to time, we saw our mother and she tried to explain what was happening and why. She told us that she was going to try to bring the three of us to live with her but it would take time before this could happen. Our mother told us she would not be living in the same house with us. She kept track of what we were doing and had asked friends to keep an eye on us. She told us to be brave and to take care of one another. She told us to always have faith that one day we would be together again.

I was not able to share my despair with anyone. Luana seemed to keep all of her thoughts to herself, and there was no communication within our household. My dad did not try to explain what was happening and spent most of his time outside, working on one thing or another. At mealtimes, we ate in silence and cleaned up without speaking. At that time, I was going to the Catholic church and learning to be an altar boy. I prayed every night using the prayers I had learned at church. I prayed for the reunion of my dad and mother. I prayed for hours. In time, I realized that my prayers were not going to be answered, and I became disillusioned. I left the church, never to return.

I found comfort only in the mountains or at the creeks where I fished. I learned to appreciate solitude and to love and admire the other beings in the forest. During my stays in the forest, I saw squirrels, chipmunks, and groundhogs. Blackbirds and swallows were always about, and crows flew by or sat high in the pines. I especially enjoyed watching hummingbirds darting through the air searching for the flowers they loved most. Sometimes I saw red-tailed hawks circling high above. I knew they were hunting for prey. I had been told they had keen eyesight and could see a mouse from that distance. Woodpeckers were always there. I thought the pecking sounds they made as they searched for insects inside the trees went well with the whistling of the wind.

Sometimes I climbed to a higher elevation. I sat and listened as the creek below plunged swiftly through a series of rocky waterfalls. The roar of the creek combined with the sounds of the wind caressing and piercing the tall pines was pleasing to me. Accompanied by the caws of crows, the hammering of woodpeckers, and the sounds of the other beings near the creek, it resembled music. Many thoughts of the forces and powers of nature and their spirits crossed my mind as I watched, and I recalled my grandfather, White Grizzly Bear. I wondered how he would cope with the problems I was experiencing now.

When I was very quiet, deer appeared to eat grass, continually alert to any danger. Sometimes, I saw a coyote quietly walking deer trails. Once, a black bear came to the creek, drank water, and ambled up the side of a steep hill. I knew there were cougar nearby, but I was never able to see one. They probably saw me.

I spent long hours of many days in the forests and returned home only when night fell. My friends in the forest knew me, I was sure, and were not disturbed by my being there.

During the summer of 1939, my dad got a job with the Works Progress Administration (wpa). Most of the work was on the reservation along the Columbia River. There were more than 300 workers, and most of them were white. It was their job to cut the trees and clear the land that was soon to be covered by water when Grand Coulee Dam was completed.

Our family followed the WPA camp every time it moved. We camped close to where the workers were clearing land so my dad could keep an eye on us. While our dad worked during the day, Luana, Bernard, and I played near our campsite with Brownie.

The Columbia River was beginning to rise. Strange things became part of the river. As we watched, old shacks or sheds slowly drifted past with the flow of the river, along with dead trees and other debris, such as the swollen corpses of cows, horses, or other animals.

The river was no longer pure and beautiful, now that it was filled with this foreign matter. In many places, the water had a muddy color. I felt that things were beginning to change. I was curious but saddened by what was taking place. At night, we could hear large chunks of the riverbanks falling into the rising water. It sounded like thunder. It was as if the river spirits were complaining about the changes that were coming.

Sometimes, my dad brought back sandwiches and cookies that were left by the workers. There were a variety of sandwiches, like beef, baloney, and peanut butter with honey. We sometimes had them for dinner or breakfast the following morning. We washed down the sandwiches with a drink from the water bag hanging from the hand crank insert bracket of the Model T. The job lasted until fall, and during that time, we camped at seven different locations in a makeshift tent our dad put together to shelter us.

After my mother separated from my dad in 1939, we did not see much of her during the remaining months of the year and most of 1940. I learned later that she had little money. She worked in restaurants in Nespelem and at Grand Coulee Dam to prepare for the divorce trial that was soon to come. She was preparing a case with an attorney she had hired in Republic, Washington, to try to gain custody of Luana, Bernard, and me.

To get from one place to another, she had to hitchhike. She did not know how to drive and could not afford the fare where buses existed. Once, she hitchhiked all the way to Missoula, Montana, to research information about my dad's past.

The trial between my dad and mother to determine who was to have custody of Luana, Bernard, and me took place in May 1940 at Republic, Washington. Luana and I understood what was taking place, and we were very uncomfortable. We did not want our dad and mother to separate, and we did not want to be part of the decision as to who we were going to live with. Bernard was only two years old and did not have any idea of what was happening.

My mother had prepared for the trial as best she could. She had a few witnesses who spoke on her behalf. She thought she had a good case, but her attorney did not represent her well. My mother lost in her attempt to win and care for us.

Judge William C. Brown ruled in favor of my dad. The court, however, realized that neither parent could properly care for the three of us. Judge Brown decided that Luana and I would be sent to an Indian boarding school off the reservation. It was further ruled that if my dad could afford it, he would have custody of the three of us during the summer. This ruling was devastating to my mother, but she was unable to contest Judge Brown's ruling. She did not have enough money to support herself and pay the legal fees to carry the fight further.

As we were getting into a friend's car to return to Inchelium after the trial, we could see our mother standing at the courthouse entrance. We saw the sadness in her face, and we felt the sadness in our hearts. We were no longer a family without our mother. We felt it would be a long time before we would be close to her again.

Judge Brown found an opening at the Chemawa Indian School in Oregon for Luana and me. He tried to get us into the DeSmet Catholic School in Idaho, but they would not take us. Since Bernard was too young for boarding school, our foster grandparents, the Halls, took care of him Mondays through Fridays while my dad worked or looked for jobs. My dad took him on weekends.

Luana and I did not know that arrangements were being made to send us away. We were busy adjusting to life without our mother. We worked together to do the chores she used to do, from cooking and cleaning house to washing clothes and caring for Bernard. We were unsure of our status and confused about what was going to happen to us.

After the household work was done and the quiet hours were upon us, we spent a lot of time reflecting on our situation. We missed the attention and care of our mother. No one stepped in to give us the teaching and guidance she had once provided. I am sure Luana missed our mother in her own way. My dad offered no explanations. Bernard sensed the unhappiness in the family and tried his best to cheer us up. He would invite Luana and me to play his favorite games of tag and hide-and-seek.

Some of my mother's items were still in the house, and when I saw them, I picked them up and held them close. A silver crucifix showing Christ hanging on the cross was on a shelf on the bedroom wall. Three large rocks still sat on the floor along the wall where my mother had left them. She had used them to warm our feet during the cold nights of winter. She did this by heating the rocks on top of the stove. When they were hot, she wrapped them in towels and placed them at the foot of our bed. Luana, Bernard, and I enjoyed the warmth, and it was always a good way to pass into sleep. These memories lingered with me, and I was briefly contented as I thought about those happier times. I remembered my mother and the good days we had when she was with us and we were a family.

Sometimes, these feelings were hard, too confusing for me. I had to leave the house and walk down to the creek and watch my fish. I could not understand why this was happening to our family. I wondered if we had done something wrong and were being punished by God and the Church. I tried to reason things out in my mind, but I could never come up with answers that satisfied me.

One day in late August 1940, our dad told Luana and me that we would be leaving home to attend school far away. I was nine years old and ready to enter the fourth grade. Luana was seven, and she would enter the second grade. That night, Luana and I packed our clothes in preparation for the trip. We did not know where the school was, but I suspected we would be gone for a long time. We were concerned about being away from Bernard for long periods, and I worried about leaving Brownie, too. But it was clear there was nothing we could do to change our situation. The problems that faced us seemed to have no answers.

I gathered up my fishing pole and all my spinners and hooks and put them in the shed. The .22 Stevens, which my dad had given me when I was eight, and what shells I had were placed under the mattress. I went down to the creek and watched the trout swimming easily by and hoped they would be all right. Ever since we came to live on the property, I never fished in our creek because I regarded the fish as my friends. Instead, I often fed them angleworms and grasshoppers.

The next day, Jess Tresseder drove up in his pickup. Jess was white, but he was part of the community. Everyone liked him, and he had two daughters about my age who were friends with us at school. The agency had arranged for Jess to transport Luana and me to the Nespelem Agency. Those who were going to the school assembled and left from there. I patted Brownie on the head, then Luana and I got into the pickup. Bernard was with our foster grandparents, the Halls, so we were not able to say good-bye to him. During the trip to Nespelem, Mr. Tresseder drove slowly so that my dad and Brownie could keep up with him in the Model T.

The trip to Nespelem took us over the old, familiar graveled road that we had traveled often. We passed a bend in Hall Creek where I had fished and where there were many crawfish. About eight miles east, we passed Twin Lakes, where we had spent days swimming and riding boats. Our family once spent the entire winter of 1935 there, living in a tent, so we would have access to the rainbow during the cold period. I remember watching my dad chopping holes in the ice with an ax and fishing for the rainbow.

Traveling higher into the mountains, we passed Gold Mountain, where we had spent the summer in 1937 when my parents were employed as fireguards. I reflected on the campsite by the road that led to the Gold Mountain lookout and thought about Pickles and the chipmunks and the happy days we had spent there. When we descended into the Sanpoil Valley and crossed Bridge Creek, I knew we were about halfway to Nespelem. We traveled south for about four miles alongside the Sanpoil River, and when we reached Cache Creek, we turned west into another mountain range. After we passed the summit, we came into open country and finally descended into the Nespelem Valley.

The trip was unpleasant for all of us. I kept looking out the rear window of the pickup to check on my dad and Brownie riding next to him in the Model T. Mr. Tresseder did not talk to us because he knew we were not in the mood and respected our feelings. The trip took nearly three hours, and when we arrived at the agency, there were several people already assembled there.

About fifteen other young people were going to make the trip to the school with Luana and me. They were staying close to their relatives and friends. I did not know any of them so I stuck close to Brownie and the Model T. Mr. Tresseder walked over and said good-bye to Luana and me. He told us to take good care of ourselves and return home safely one day. Mr. Tresseder walked over to my dad and talked a while. He shook my dad's hand, got into his pickup, and drove away.

After being checked in by a tribal official, those of us who were leaving exchanged good-byes with our friends and relatives. I hugged Brownie and climbed into the truck after Luana, who was lifted in by the driver. The sides and back of the truck's cargo area were constructed of posts and crosspieces. You could see out even if you were sitting on the bed of the truck. The two men in the cab took turns driving during the trip.

We were on our way at about 4:30 in the afternoon, and the weather was pleasant. I could recognize the area we were traveling through as we passed by Grand Coulee Dam. I thought of Harry Wong and the restaurant on B Street where he had prepared tasty but unusual meals for Luana and me. I recalled the sweets and fruits from China, with their wonderful but strange tastes. I also thought of the pretty women who always greeted and talked with Luana and me. After we passed through the town, we were in unfamiliar country.

As darkness came, we tried to make ourselves comfortable by sitting and then lying on the bed of the truck. After a while, I fell asleep, and when I awoke, I felt cold and hungry. My light jacket gave me some relief, but there was no food in the truck, so I dismissed the feeling of hunger and tried to think of something else. Luana was sitting across from me on the bed of the truck. I could see that she was cold, too. She had a worried look on her face. She seemed to be concentrating on something personal. I wanted to talk to her, but I could not think of anything to say.

As the truck drove on, I saw new country. I did not know how long the trip would take or where we were going. When we reached a wooded area, the truck stopped and the driver told us to get out and relieve ourselves if we had to. I ran to the nearest clump of bushes next to some trees, as did everyone else. I was glad it was dark because this gave us some privacy.

After we had finished, we climbed into the back of the truck and tried to make ourselves comfortable and get some sleep. I managed to sleep off and on, but I was awakened by the cold. The sides of the truck were not designed to block the wind, and we all had difficulty keeping warm.

The results of our parents' separation and the trial were very hard on Luana and me. Our cold journey to a faraway destination ended a familiar way of life we had learned to love. Our family was lost, and we were beginning to lose our culture and the closeness of tribal life. We faced a new life full of uncertainties and challenges. It seemed to me that the future held little promise. There was nothing left to look forward to.

7 / Chemawa

We arrived at Chemawa Indian School sometime in the early morning, when it was still dark. A person came out of a building and separated us according to sex. I could see the fear and uncertainty in Luana's eyes. I did not know how to help or comfort her. We were led to different buildings. Once inside, we were assigned to rooms that had four cots each. We were told to get some sleep. Luana and I had not eaten since noon of the day before, and I was more hungry than sleepy. The buildings and campus were foreign to me, and I was apprehensive about being there. I did not know anyone I could confide in, so I got into bed without undressing and went to sleep.

When we woke later that morning, without having breakfast, we were taken to another building, where ten older girls waited. They had prepared a solution of vinegar, water, and other ingredients to wash our hair. This mixture would rid us of lice if we had them. The girls were efficient, and I thought they must have done this often.

I was surprised to see so many Indians. They were of different ages. They were everywhere. They smiled as they saw us being shampooed by the older girls. We were embarrassed at being handled in this manner. I had never had my hair washed by a stranger, and I was apprehensive about being touched by someone outside my family. Only my mother had done this, and always in a caring and gentle manner.

After the girls washed our hair, we were taken back to the dormitories and told to undress and take showers. I had never showered before, and I enjoyed the water as it washed over my body. Next, we were taken to another building and given very short haircuts. Then, we returned to our dorms and received our new clothes. The pants, shirts, and jackets were of blue denim. The school also provided us with underwear—white shorts and undershirts—black high-top shoes, and black socks. We were told to change into our new clothes. We were all dressed alike, and we seemed to all look alike. I was happy with the new clothes and shoes, but hunger was uppermost in my mind. Before we left for our rooms, we each received a comb, a toothbrush, and a paper sack of tooth powder. It was close to noon before we were finally taken to the mess hall for something to eat.

Within the next five to six days, other Indian students arrived from other tribes. Some wore moccasins and a number wore braids. I could not distinguish the different tribes, but I learned later that the students came from Alaska, California, Idaho, Montana, Oregon, and Washington.

I learned that some arrived at Chemawa without shoes. My shoes were old and worn, and I was close to growing out of them, but at least I had shoes. I felt fortunate. I didn't have very much, but I realized now that others had less. The clothing of most of the students was old and worn. Many had holes in their clothes. Some had patches on their pants and shirts.

I became aware that most of the students came to Chemawa because of problems at home. Some came from homes broken by divorce, like Luana and me. Others were forced to leave because of deaths in their families, when their guardians could no longer afford to keep them. Lack of money was always the root of the many problems. All of us were poor, and our families were unable to support us.

I was impressed with the number of Indians who were assembling at Chemawa. By the time everyone was assigned to a dorm and classes were about to begin, the number of students had grown to more than 800. The students were of various ages and represented grades one through twelve.

At first, the students of each tribe stayed close together. Some conversed only in their own language. There were sullen looks all around. Most of us had never met people from other tribes. We were strangers to one another.

As days turned into weeks, tribal barriers began to break down, and we began to communicate. We were curious about the places everyone had left behind and made efforts to get to know one another. We came to understand that we all had something in common, regardless of our tribal backgrounds. Friendships formed. It was as if a new tribe was developing.

After a few weeks had gone by, I had met many boys my age and learned of tribes that I had never heard of before. I could relate easily enough to those who came from inland tribes whose environments were similar to mine, but others from the coastal areas along the shores of the Pacific Ocean seemed different. This might have been caused by their different customs and ways of life. The students from California also did not act or look like those from the Plateau. I got to know a boy from Alaska who looked like pictures I had seen in books and magazines. His name was Noel. He was the first Eskimo I had ever met. He had a strange way of talking, but I could understand him if I listened carefully. At times, he spoke his native language, which sounded very strange to me.

I met boys my age from several tribes, and they became my friends. Curtis was a Fort Hall Indian, and Howard was from Bay Center on the coast of Washington State. Robert was a Yakama, Louis a Nez Perce, and Dopey from the Umatilla Tribe. I never learned Dopey's real name. His nickname fit him well because he had big ears. He did not mind being called that name by someone he liked, but if people who weren't his friends tried it, he would punch them. He was very good at fighting, and he could hit very hard. Donald, Francis, and Tommy were Colvilles, but I had not known them before Chemawa. They had come to Chemawa a few years before me, when they were very young.

At Chemawa, I could see that almost everything was different. There were no pine trees like we had back home. The trees that stood at random about the campus were maple, walnut, birch, tall fir, and cedar. The main dormitory buildings and large mess hall were made of dark red brick. These buildings were surrounded by lawns and connected by a crisscrossing of concrete sidewalks.

I found out later that there were more than seventy buildings in Chemawa. Several, like the hospital, auditorium, and classrooms, were east of the railroad tracks. The store, post office, and railroad station were also on the east side of the campus. All the dormitories and the mess hall were west of the railroad tracks. The buildings where many of the trades were taught were located to the south, near the football field and track. These buildings were large and housed a variety of machines and equipment that were used by the older students as they learned different trades. South of the campus was a graveyard. There were nearly 300 markers there. This was the final resting place for students of many tribes who did not return to their homelands.

The buildings at Chemawa were surrounded by 450 acres of land. A variety of crops was grown during the summer. There were also fruit orchards and fields of alfalfa that provided feed for the cattle. A tall red water tower stood east of the campus. The word "Chemawa" was painted in big white capital letters on the tank. Chemawa, I learned, was six miles north of Salem, Oregon. It was an off-reservation Indian boarding school designed to separate Indian children from their native culture. The school's main purpose was to force Indian children into the mainstream of white American culture.

Years later, I would realize that the layout and landscaping of

Chemawa resembled small New England universities. For the first time in my life, I was to study, learn, and live in buildings that had electricity, running water, and indoor plumbing. Heat was piped through the buildings and dispersed throughout the rooms by radiators placed near the windows. This way of living was a new experience for everyone I knew at Chemawa.

The weather at Chemawa was different from what I was used to in Inchelium. The air was moist, and when fall and winter came, there was no snow, only rain. Weather conditions were not easily predicted, and pleasant days occurred unexpectedly during the winter months. The weather did not get down to freezing during the winter, so the jackets we wore kept us warm on cold days.

The younger boys close to my age were assigned rooms in Brewer Hall. Each room provided space for four boys. Each student had a small cot, a small table and a chair, and an open closet with shelves that were designed to hold extra clothes and any personal belongings.

The matron's assistant walked down the halls ringing a bell to awaken us at 5:00 A.M. He taught us how to make our cots in military style. We made our cots before we were assembled and marched to the mess hall for breakfast at 6:00 A.M.

After breakfast, we went back to our rooms, where we brushed our teeth with a mixture of baking soda and powdered toothpaste. We combed our hair and brushed our clothes to make sure they were clean. We wiped our shoes clean with a damp cloth and shined them with black shoe polish. Afterward, we assembled in the entrance hallway and marched to classes at 9:00 A.M.

At 12:00 noon, we were marched to the mess hall for the midday meal, then marched back to classes at 1:00 P.M. Classes were over at 4:00 P.M. Marching to the mess hall for supper took place at 6:00 P.M. We were allowed free time until 8:30 P.M. The matron's assistant's bell signaled us to retire for the evening, and all lights had to be out at 8:45 P.M.

The boys cleaned and maintained the dorm themselves under the direction of the matron and her assistant. The washroom, lavatories, showers, bedrooms, hallways, and entry were thoroughly cleaned on Saturdays. After the floors were cleaned and mopped, they were waxed. The floors were polished with rags placed underfoot as dozens of students worked in all directions. We dusted all flat surfaces with damp cloths and then wiped the areas dry. The windows were washed until they were spotless. The matron inspected the entire dorm in the late afternoon. If conditions met her approval, we were allowed the rest of the day off, but the cleaning usually continued until Sunday.

Sunday night was shower night for all of us in the dorm. To make sure we were clean, the matron's assistant checked us after we got out of the showers. He was a short, muscular, red-haired man in his late 20s. He seemed to enjoy his power over small boys. He would stand in a cocky manner at the entrance to the shower room, holding a large brush designed to scrub floors. When he found boys who had not done a good job, he grabbed them and vigorously brushed the areas of their bodies that were not clean. He especially enjoyed scrubbing ears. He would grab offenders by the hair, yank them toward him, and brush their ears so forcefully they sometimes bled.

I observed this treatment many times, but I never saw anyone cry. We were determined to hold our own and never cry out in pain or ask for his mercy. When he was nearby, there was always tension. There was no respect. We considered him the enemy. No one liked him, but we were too small and too young to do anything about it.

The matron's assistant displayed his arrogance daily. It was obvious that he did not like us. His manner was always abusive. His treatment of us, however, did not lower our pride or self-respect. I believe we all appreciated the fact that we tolerated the assistant and his mistreatment within our own dorm. We did not seek help from the older boys, who stayed in another dorm called McNary Hall. When we talked about the matron's assistant, we did it in hushed tones. We tried to avoid him and grew to dislike him very much.

One Sunday night, after he was particularly abusive, we got together and talked about beating him up. We knew he was strong, but we felt that if enough of us jumped him, we could win. When older boys at Brewer Hall heard about our plans, they persuaded us to forget about it. They convinced us that we would get everyone in Brewer Hall into serious trouble. We thought about their advice and decided they were right. This ended our plans for ambushing the matron's assistant, and we endured his abuse until the school year ended and he left.

The matron did not seem happy. She never smiled and regarded us with contempt. She never touched us, and when she spoke to us, she did not make eye contact. She did not seem to consider us human beings. I now think she thought we were inferior and had to be managed like "wildlife."

When she talked to her assistant, she did not look at him either. She issued orders for the day and depended on him to carry them out. Sometimes, we would see her and pass by her outside the dorm, but she never looked at us or greeted us. It was as if we did not exist. The matron spent most of her time in her office inside the dorm. I do not recall her receiving visitors.

The teachers were more considerate. Although they were white, they seemed interested in helping us learn. Some of the teachers went out of their way to help. They understood that some students needed more help than others and adjusted their ways of teaching to get this done. However, teachers and students did not establish close relationships. The teachers had a job to do, and they did it. After class hours, they were not seen. Because they were unavailable, we had no one to confide in or turn to for advice. Since we all faced this problem, we learned to depend on one another for support and backing. We were to become very close as time went by.

At night, before falling asleep, I often had many thoughts of home. The welfare of Bernard and Brownie would occupy my thoughts. I did not know it then, but Bernard was having a difficult time. He lived five days a week with his foster grandparents, the Halls, because my dad had to work at a variety of jobs wherever he could find them. Food was hard to come by, and Bernard didn't have fresh milk. When my dad could afford it, Bernard drank canned milk mixed with water. During the winter, food became very hard to find, and there were no vegetables or fruit.

Because the Halls were elderly, it was hard for them to give Bernard the care and companionship he needed. He spent most of his time indoors because they were not in good health and preferred to stay inside. Since there were no other children nearby, Bernard did not have the advantage of learning to relate to others his own age. He had no toys, and he had to improvise ways to entertain himself. My mother was supporting herself by working in restaurants in Nespelem and at Grand Coulee Dam. She was far away and could not care for him when he needed it. Bernard did not have the opportunity to enjoy the attention and instruction Luana and I received when our mother was with us.

The dry air and the smell of the pine trees did not exist in Chemawa. I missed the sound of the creek flowing past our house and the forests, mountains, and streams where I used to fish. I also missed the strong winds that blew through the canyon at Hall Creek and the way their good advice always came to me when we talked.

Chemawa's location in relation to my homeland was still unknown to me, and I had no idea of how far I was from home. I did not know how long I would be in Chemawa. Sometimes I wondered if I would ever see home again. These were disturbing thoughts, so I decided I would try to make the best of it, hoping that the future would be better.

A few weeks had gone by, and I realized that I had not seen Luana in all that time. I decided to make a point of asking the matron if she could tell me of her welfare. The matron told me abruptly that Luana was in the McBride dormitory and that it was not my business to be concerned about others.

We marched back and forth to classes in other buildings and to the mess hall for meals. We did not exactly display military precision, but as time went on, we began to look better. It became routine to assemble in formation and then march to classes, the mess, athletic contests, and other important events. We saw the young girls from time to time as they walked in large groups to the mess hall and classrooms. At times, I saw Luana walking with the other girls. She always looked worried. She never smiled. We looked at each other, but we never got close enough to talk. The older students did not have to march and were allowed to walk around the campus at will.

After we arrived at our first class and before we were allowed to sit, we had to stand in line to take our daily dose of cod liver oil. The teacher gave us each a tablespoon of the medicine followed by a slice of orange to help ease the taste. None of us liked this way of beginning class, but there was no avoiding it. The cod liver oil must have worked for me. I don't remember having one cold during the time I was in Chemawa. Years later, after I left Chemawa, I would think of cod liver oil and experience the taste every time I ate an orange.

One day, the matron told me I was to go to the hospital that night and should take my toothbrush and comb with me. She said her assistant would walk me to the hospital after dinner at the mess hall. I found out that five other boys from my dorm were going to the hospital, too.

While we were waiting for the matron's assistant, we asked one another why we were going to the hospital. No one knew. The matron did not tell us why we were going. We found out that none of us had ever been to a hospital before. We did not know what to expect. We knew that people who were sick had to go to the hospital, but all six of us were well, with no sign of illness.

The matron's assistant walked us the short distance to the hospital. No one talked. A nurse met us at the entrance and gave us each a nightgown. She showed us our beds and said that was where we would sleep while we were there. The nurse told us to put on the nightgowns, and then she left. We all started laughing because we thought we looked funny in the nightgowns. The nurse returned and put small glass stems in our mouths. I learned later that these were thermometers. One boy asked the nurse why we were in the hospital, and she told us that we were going to have our tonsils removed. None of us knew what tonsils were, and I could tell that we were all concerned. We did not know where the tonsils were and whether the operation to remove them was going to be painful. The nurse told us to get into bed.

About a half hour went by, and another nurse brought a bed on wheels into our room. She asked one boy to lie down on the bed. After he was in position, she pushed him out of the room. Less than half an hour later, the nurse returned with the boy on the wheeled bed. He was asleep. Two nurses put him back into his bed. Another boy was told to get onto the bed with wheels and was taken out of the room. While the nurses were gone, two boys walked over to the sleeping student. They told the rest of us that he smelled funny and his eyes were only half closed.

One by one, the rest of us were wheeled out of the room and came back asleep. I was the fifth to be wheeled out. When I got into what was the operating room, a doctor told me he was going to put me to sleep. He told me not to worry about anything. He said he was going to put some ether over my nose and I should breathe deeply. The ether smelled strange. The next thing I knew, I was waking up in my bed with a slight headache and a sore throat. I could not swallow. None of us could talk, and we all had sore throats. We stayed in the hospital for about three days. The matron's assistant walked us back to the dorm afterward. I thought to myself that the hospital was a better place to be. The food was better. The nurses were friendly, and there was no matron's assistant to worry about. Weeks later, I found out that every boy my age who roomed in Brewer Hall had lost his tonsils.

In the mess hall, younger students ate with older students at large round tables that seated eight. This was done so that the older students could teach the younger ones table manners. A bell rang to signal the beginning of mess and a bell rang to signal the end of mess. The mess hall was very large and could seat more than 1,000 people. As soon as mess commenced, there was a steady roar from the sound of all the students and personnel eating at once.

Although there was supervision from the older students, it was every man for himself at the table. We learned to eat a variety of foods. We seemed to need the energy they provided. We were constantly involved in some activity at Chemawa and must have burned a lot of energy.

We all seemed to get hungry at night, so we learned to make sandwiches of mashed potatoes or beans flavored with salt and pepper. We wrapped them in napkins, hid them in our pockets, and took them back to the dorm after mess. Before bedtime, we warmed the sandwiches on top of the radiators if the weather was cold. If the weather was warm, we ate the sandwiches as they were. This helped satisfy our hunger until breakfast the next morning. I remember the older students at the table smiling at us while we prepared our sandwiches. I assume they had probably done the same thing when they were younger.

No one seemed to suffer from boredom. The days held much that was of interest to us, and time went by quickly. Some of us acquired a taste for coffee. Several did not care for the cocoa that was served at breakfast on certain days. Those of us who grew to love coffee could not wait for the days when it was served.

One Saturday, when we had finished cleaning the dorm, I was standing in the courtyard. Howard, Curtis, Donald, and Dopey were there with me. Howard said, "I wish I had a cup of coffee. I really miss it when we don't have it at mess."

"I miss it, too," Donald agreed. "I used to always have coffee at home."

Dopey said, "Let's buy some. I know how to make it. I made it all the time for my dad and brother."

"I have fifteen cents," I offered. "How much does it cost?"

Francis walked up and suggested that if we all put in a little money, we might have enough to buy some. We searched our pockets and found some coins to put in Dopey's hand. "Let's go to the store and see if we have enough," said Francis.

Dopey and Francis went into the store. They came out and told the rest of us that they didn't have enough money. "How much more do we need?" I asked. Francis answered that we needed thirty-five cents. Robert, Leo, and Louis walked up, and Dopey asked, "Do you guys have any money? We want to buy some coffee, and we don't have enough money." Robert, Leo, and Louis dug into their pockets and came up with a total of thirty cents. "We need five cents more," said Dopey.

Tommy came walking up, and Francis asked him if he had a nickel. "Yes," Tommy answered, "but I'm going to buy some candy." Francis, who was Tommy's older brother, ordered Tommy to give him the nickel. "We need coffee more than you need candy," he said. Tommy thought a while and realized that he liked coffee, too. He also did not want to make Francis angry. So he handed over the coin.

We could only afford a small sack. We got matches at the store and a gallon can from the mess hall, and an older student gave us a jug to hold water. Then, since Dopey knew how to make coffee, he took charge.

He led us to a heavily wooded area about a half mile from the campus. As we walked, we could see houses in the distance. Dopey told us that we were not allowed to go near those houses. He said white people lived there, and they did not want Indians near their property. Dopey added that if we were caught near the houses of the white people, we would be reported to the matron.

I was pleased by the density of the woods. The fir trees were tall, and once we were deep into the woods, it gave us a feeling of privacy. The feeling reminded me of home, when I had gone into the forest to escape and think. As I walked with my friends, I thought about my grandfather, White Grizzly Bear. It seemed his presence was near every time I was deep in the woods. I felt more at home in Chemawa with these thoughts.

In the wooded area, we gathered some wood and made a fire around three large rocks. Dopey placed the gallon can on the rocks and poured water into the can from the jug. The water quickly came to a boil, and Dopey poured in coffee from the sack. He picked up a small branch and stirred the coffee and boiling water. The first batch of coffee was weak, so Dopey added more coffee the next time. The second batch proved to be good, and we enjoyed our first "coffee break."

Making and drinking coffee became a Saturday afternoon ritual. The number of coffee drinkers grew to more than a dozen. While we sat around the fire and drank the coffee, we talked about a variety of subjects.

One Saturday, after enjoying our coffee, Donald asked Dopey what his reservation looked like. Dopey answered, "Our land is near the Columbia River in Oregon. During the summer, it gets very hot, and during the winter, there is snow. There are not very many trees near the river, but there is a lot of sagebrush. There are big rocks on the land and in the river. There are deer and jackrabbits. We also have a lot of rattlesnakes."

Dopey set his small tin drinking can next to the fire, stood, and walked deeper into the woods. He returned with several dry limbs and threw a few into the fire. Then he continued, "When the salmon run, many of our people fish in the Columbia. Some go downriver and fish at Celilo. There are many salmon there, and people of different tribes fish there. One year, I went with my dad and brothers, and I met and made friends with some Yakimas. There were others—I think they were Wishrams. They also live along the Columbia River. I would eat a lot of dried salmon. They go good with camas and huckleberries."

Robert said, "On the Yakima, it also gets hot in the summer, and the winters are cold. We live close to the Yakima River. At Mount Adams, there are a lot of trees, and there are deer and elk up there. That's about all that everyone eats except for the salmon that are caught at Celilo Falls. There are a lot of huckleberries at Mount Adams, and everyone goes up in August to pick them. Everyone likes them, and sometimes people stay more than a week in the mountains. There are a lot of coyotes, bear, and rattlesnakes, too. Near the lakes, you can see bald eagles swooping down to catch fish. It's beautiful in the mountains."

Robert shifted from a sitting to a kneeling position. "I have also been to Celilo," he continued. "I like to watch the salmon jump the falls. When they can't make it, they fall back into the traps. Those that clear the falls go upriver. The salmon are very large. They are my best food. I like to eat them with fry bread and wild honey."

"At Bay Center in Washington, we live near the ocean," Howard began. "Many of our tribe fish for salmon. We also go out and get clams. I don't remember any snow, but it gets cold in the winter and it rains a lot. We have a lot of seagulls. There are also deer but I have never seen any elk or coyotes. I have never seen any rattlesnakes, but I think I saw an eagle once. When you walk the beaches, you can see jellyfish and crabs and starfish." Howard rose, then knelt and reached for the gallon can of coffee balanced on the three large rocks. He poured more coffee into his small drinking can. He continued, "I have heard there are killer whales in the ocean. I have never seen them, but I have seen pictures. I have also seen woodcarvings, and they have one high fin on their backs. They are black and white in color and eat seals and salmon. They swim very fast, and they can jump out of the water easily. I have heard that they are friends of the People. Our people have much respect for them."

I told Robert, "Your land is probably like mine. The Okanogan River borders our reservation on the west. The Columbia River with Kettle Falls flows on the eastern side and also borders it on the south. At Kettle Falls, there are strong spirits that help our people. We have a lot of streams and lakes, and they all have fish like mountain trout, rainbow, and eastern brook. I really enjoy being near the streams. I like the sounds as they turn into falls and flow past the large rocks."

Howard handed Curtis the gallon can of coffee. Curtis filled his drinking can and placed the gallon can back onto the three large rocks. He set his drinking can next to the fire and sat cross-legged near it. "We have spirits back home," he said. "They are in the mountains and the woods. Sometimes they can be found in the river also." Curtis paused, then asked, "Do you have any great leaders or warriors in your tribes?"

Robert answered, "My tribe had many great warriors, and Kamiakin was a great chief. We fought the white man and killed many of them when they tried to invade our homeland."

"The Colvilles and Lakes did not go to war with the whites," I added, "but they did kill white miners when they started digging up the land, looking for gold, along the Columbia River. They were warned to stay off our land, but they continued to come, so our warriors killed them."

Louis spoke up. "We fought the whites. We had no choice. They made us leave our land at the Wallowa. They attacked us, and we fought back. We tried to avoid warfare and escape to Canada, but they sent soldiers to kill us. They would not let us go. We won most of the battles, but we ran out of chiefs, warriors, and finally food and ammunition. Chief Joseph lost his younger brother, Ollicut, the leader of the young men. Looking Glass, one of our best war chiefs, was also killed. We even lost women and children. The whites are not honorable in war. They kill the helpless."

Louis stood up. He emptied his drinking can and placed it near the fire. He stretched with his fingers clenched and locked behind his neck, then walked deep into the woods.

All of us sitting around the small campfire nodded. We were angry. Regardless of our tribal background, we all respected and admired Chief

Joseph. We drank coffee for several minutes in silence, respecting the memory of Joseph, Ollicut, and the Nez Perce.

During those early days, we did not have drums, so those who knew how to sing and drum would pound with smaller sticks on a large tree limb. Some of the boys who could dance showed us the steps of certain dances. They explained that tribes like the Spokanes, Yakimas, and Nez Perce used the round bustle style of war dance. They also performed the steps of the Owl Dance, Swan Dance, and Butterfly Dance. A Nez Perce said that he knew the Sneak-up Dance and performed the steps of crouching and kneeling. This, he said, was a Plains War Dance. A boy from Bellingham, who was a Lummi, showed the steps that were used in the Eagle and Wolf Dances. Another, from the Fort Hall Reservation in Idaho, said they used different songs and steps when they did the Eagle and Wolf Dances. He went on to say that his favorite dance was the Hoop Dance. I had never heard of such a dance, and many years would go by before I finally saw it performed.

We also talked about the animals that lived in our homelands. We all had respect for rattlesnakes. Animals that preyed on others—such as bear, cougar, wolf, and coyote— fascinated us. We all knew that the grizzly was the most dangerous. We had seen eagles and hawks capture prey back home, and we admired them. Some students from Montana and the Dakotas told about the buffalo, pronghorn antelope, and wolves that lived in their homelands. It was clear that we loved animals as much as we loved people. We believed that animals were people also, another type of people.

I remembered my mother telling me that the Sin-Aikst regarded the other beings as equal to people and always felt a deep respect for them. The People knew that the beings held special power. Sometimes a person took the name of a being, like White Grizzly Bear did, and was called by that name for the rest of his life. It was believed that shamans could change from one of the People into a being, and then back to one of the People again. Only shamans held these special powers.

Some talked about how tepees were set up. Others explained how hand drums were made and decorated. A few described how to skin deer and prepare the hide that would be made into buckskin. Our tribes had various ways of preparing salmon for drying and smoking, but we all agreed on how to dry and smoke deer meat and dry huckleberries. Those from coastal tribes like the Lummi, Makah, and Quinault talked about seafood such as clams and strange fish that came from the ocean. A boy from the Makah Reservation said his people used to go out in their canoes to kill whales. He said they would bring the whales back to the village, divide the meat equally, and eat it.

It was during these times that I learned about other Indians and their ways of living. I also heard about how different tribes dealt with the everyday challenge of surviving on land changed and controlled by another people with a different culture. I learned about their history and something about the leaders of these tribes.

These experiences helped me develop for the first time the feeling of being an Indian. Back home, I did not think of myself or our people as Indian. I knew, from what my mother told me, that we were once called Sin-Aikst. Now that we were called Lakes, much of our Indian ways had ended. Drumming or singing was not heard. I do not remember seeing traditional dancing. Fine beadwork or featherwork was rare. In short, the culture of the Inchelium area had changed, and most of the people had adopted white ways in their struggle to survive.

Our coffee-drinking regulars were soon joined by a much larger group of students our age. The wooded area where we met to make and drink coffee was large. One day, a Nez Perce suggested we play war. "Like our tribes used to fight?" asked a Shoshone. And a Puyallup added, "What kind of weapons can we use?"

"We can make bows and arrows," said a Warm Springs. "I know how to make them." A Blackfeet said he knew how to make war clubs, and a Klamath told us it was easy to make lances. Another student, a Spokane, wondered what rules we should fight by. "We will fight and ambush, and we will divide equally," replied a Coeur d'Alene. And a Quinault added, "We will fight, but we will not kill." The boys agreed to the rules of war, and we all went to work making weapons.

The heavy growth of bushes and trees were ideal for hiding and setting up ambushes. The weapons would be lances made from poles, bows and blunt-pointed arrows, war clubs, and rocks. Those who were fortunate enough to think of it collected garbage can lids to use as shields.

Boys, who happened to be in the woods on a Saturday, were divided into two sides. Sometimes more than a hundred boys played. The strategy and maneuvers were well planned and executed during the games. It was not uncommon for someone to get hurt. Rocks hit their targets, leaving many with bumps and bruises. Knives, lances, and war clubs produced punctures, bruises, and lacerations. Sometimes anger and bad feelings resulted. We learned how to deal with pain. We learned much about strategy, tactics, and battle. After the war games, we doctored our wounds with iodine. One of the boys had gotten a bottle from a cousin who lived in McNary Hall. Afterward, we carefully hid our weapons in the bushes and returned the garbage can lids. We wanted to keep them safe for the next war games. We engaged in these games often during my first year at Chemawa.

Sometimes I witnessed the loneliness of friends and other boys at Chemawa, but they did not talk out loud about their feelings. They did not share their innermost feelings with anyone. Years of deprivation had toughened them. When feelings of loneliness became overpowering, those afflicted would go off by themselves and bear their anguish in private.

The only time I heard words of loneliness was when we gathered on Saturdays for our coffee breaks in the woods. After we had exhausted the topics of various Indian ways and experiences, someone would talk about the people he missed. Our carefree and happy attitudes were set aside as we sat quietly and thought about loved ones and home.

Those who had no families or homes of their own listened quietly to the expressions of loneliness. Accepting their situation, they put aside deep feelings of family, friends, and home. They would not allow painful feelings to surface and interfere with the new lifestyle that had been thrust upon them at Chemawa.

Mail from home did not come often. At times, some students would get packages filled with traditional foods from home. I had made friends with a few Yakamas, and when they received food from home, they invited me to eat with them. The packages contained dried foods such as deer meat, salmon, and huckleberries as well as camas roots and finger bread.

We found that the sharing and eating of traditional food was the next best thing to being home. Warm feelings of family, friends, and the People as a whole crossed our minds as we ate. The food satisfied more than our physical cravings. It gave us the strength to endure. Sharing helped us realize that we all had something in common. Although we came from many tribes, we were in essence transformed into one tribe while in the confines of Chemawa. We understood this as we tried to cope with and survive the dictates of a people who did not understand us or the cultures we came from. Sharing this food gave us good feelings, and the friendships we established then continue to this day. One Yakima friend from Chemawa became a leader of his people in later life. His name was Robert Jim.

There was little contact with home. As time went by, Chemawa became my home away from home. We adjusted to the school schedule and anticipated the events that interested us most. All activities were self-contained. We had no contacts outside the boundaries of Chemawa except for athletic contests.

During my first year at Chemawa, I left the campus only once. In the middle of October 1940, our mother paid Luana and me an unexpected visit. We were both surprised and very happy. Our mother was given permission to take us off-campus for one day. We walked the one mile to Kickback and caught a bus to Salem, Oregon, which was six miles south.

My mother took Luana to have her hair cut and curled. While this was taking place, she took me to a restaurant for something to eat. She asked if I was treated well at Chemawa. I told her everything was fine but a lot different from home. I added that I had made several friends from different tribes. I went on to say that I had never seen so many Indians before. I mentioned that I was learning about many tribes and how they lived on their reservations. I told her that some of my new friends were like us but others had customs that were strange to me.

After we finished eating, we brought Luana some take-out in a box. Then we walked around Salem, window-shopped, and went to a matinee movie. We returned by bus to Kickback. The three of us walked the one mile to Chemawa as the sun was setting.

While we were visiting with our mother, we had much to share of our experiences in Chemawa. She listened quietly as we talked and then offered us advice on how to get along better. Luana asked our mother about home and how Bernard and Brownie were. She said she missed Bernard and wished she could return home to be close to him. Luana added that someone should be at home to help our dad take care of Bernard.

Visiting with our mother reminded us of past times. It gave us great comfort to receive direction from my mother again. She made the future seem brighter. We were reminded of our closeness with her. We had not seen her for five months, and we tried to make the best of what we knew would be a short visit.

It was time to go back to our dorms, so my mother hugged Luana and me. She held us close to her. We all had tears in our eyes as we said our good-byes. She left us at our dorms and then walked back to Kickback to catch a bus that would eventually take her home. We were not to see her again for three years, after we had returned to the reservation.

In November, other visitors surprised me. Jess Tresseder, his wife, and two daughters were passing through on their way to Inchelium. They made it a point to stop at Chemawa to visit me. I got into their car because it was raining, and we drove around the campus. I showed them all the points of interest: the dorms, the mess hall, the auditorium, the classrooms, and the buildings where the trades were taught. I also showed them the hospital and the athletic field where football games were played.

We talked for about an hour, and Mr. Tresseder said that my dad and Bernard were doing well but that they missed Luana and me. He told me he and his family were on their way back to Inchelium. He said he would tell my dad he had seen us and that we were well. We said goodbye. It was heartwarming to see someone from home. I was grateful that they had taken the time to visit me.

Visits from parents, relatives, or friends were rare. There was usually no contact with people from home until after nine months had gone by. Students who came from totally broken homes remained in Chemawa until relatives could afford to adopt them. Sometimes, students became so homesick that they would run away. Runaways were usually older students who knew where they were going. They would catch a railroad car on a slow-moving freight train that reduced its speed when it was passing through Chemawa. Most of us younger students did not know where our homes were or which direction we should take to get there. We never thought seriously about running away.

Additional cleaning of the dorm and other buildings was the punishment for any infractions of the rules at Chemawa. The matron's assistant was always able to find more areas that needed cleaning. When the infractions were more serious, the offender had to run through the belt line. About twenty-four or thirty students would remove their belts and form two lines. The offender had to run between the lines, and the members of the belt line struck his back and legs as he ran through.

The matron's assistant was always present to make sure the students in the belt line did their job and did not hold back when swinging their belts. It was obvious that he enjoyed watching pain being inflicted on others. Although this type of punishment left only minor injuries, it was never a pleasant experience for the offender. It was a good bet that the offender would not do anything to warrant running the belt line any time soon.

I did not experience any harsh restraint against Indian culture or tradition at Chemawa. Generations of Indians before me had already felt the full force of that practice. I learned that in earlier years, speaking the Indian language had been forbidden. White authority had dealt harshly with Indian dancing, singing, and drumming. Students were not allowed to braid their hair or wear any ornaments with Indian design motifs. During my time, efforts to teach the white way were still in force, but attempts to abolish or restrain Indian culture were past. The practice of Indian culture, however, was not encouraged or discussed.

One man, Captain Richard Henry Pratt (later Brigadier General) of the U.S. Army, believed differently from most whites of the late 1800s. He felt that Indians could become part of the nation's move toward change. Pratt also believed that the Indian culture and ways of living were inferior to white ways and that Indians had to be "civilized." Indian ways had to be killed to save the Indian people. Pratt also believed Indian boarding schools could not succeed if they were located on reservations and should instead be at great distances from the reservations. He further believed that the Indians' inferiority was cultural not racial. In other words, the difference between a savage and a civilized man could be explained by environment. Richard Henry Pratt (later known as the "father" of Indian education) convinced the government that he was right and received approval to create the Carlisle Indian School near Harrisburg, Pennsylvania, in 1879. Carlisle was the first off-reservation Indian boarding school in the United States.

On February 25, 1880, Chemawa Indian School became the second off-reservation Indian boarding school. Its original location was Forest Grove, Oregon, and its initial enrollment was eighteen students. Chemawa remained at Forest Grove until 1885, when, because of the growing number of students, the school had to expand or move. The administrators decided to build a larger school with more acreage.

Chemawa opened at its new site in 1885. The new location was on 450 acres of land six miles north of Salem, Oregon. The school proved to be very successful, and by 1926, enrollment was more than 1,000 students. Chemawa was designed to be a vocational-trade school, and its emphasis was on training both the mind and the hand. The school was self-contained, a small world within itself.

Vocational training was extensive, and many students benefited from what they learned at Chemawa. Classes were offered to prepare for the following positions: auto mechanic, barber or beautician, blacksmith, business owner, carpenter, chef, dairy worker, electrician, farmer, gardener, home nurse, janitor, laundry or dry cleaner operator, leather worker, machinist, painter, plumber, printer, sheet-metal worker, shoemaker, spotter, stationary engineer, tailor or seamstress, waitperson, and welder. Courses were also taught in homemaking, Indian arts, and college prep.

Each course was designed to cover four years. Half of each day was spent in specific study of the chosen trade and the other half in academic study.

The name "Chemawa" came from the Calapooia Tribe, which was located near Albany, Oregon, near the Willamette River. The word originally meant "desolate," but the name later came to mean "happy home." Chemawa became a happy home to thousands of Indians, many of whom came from totally broken homes, even today. The extent and caliber of training and the student response to it have never been greater than they were in the 1940s.

The younger boys were in awe of the older ones who excelled in athletics. The best players in each sport were called all-stars, and they were the heroes of the Chemawa campus. For many years, Chemawa fielded strong teams in football, track, basketball, boxing, and wrestling. When we realized how strong our teams were, we became the most supportive fans. We knew each player's strong points, and we could often predict what each player would do against Chemawa's opponents.

Excitement was at its highest when we hosted other teams on our home field. The school band dressed in red-and-white uniforms added to our excitement by playing the Chemawa fight song. Many of us felt that our team represented the Indian warriors fighting the cavalry when they took the field. Successes on the "battlefield" strengthened many and took our minds off our feelings of homesickness. The successes also gave us pride and prepared us to face a life dominated by white values.

When we saw our backfield make great runs or cross the goal line for touchdowns, we thought about the Carlisle football player Jim Thorpe. We knew that Thorpe was a Potawatomie Sac-Fox Indian and that he was considered the world's greatest athlete. We could identify with him and admire him for what he'd gone through and what he became.

Another great athlete at Carlisle was Alex Arcasa, a Lakes Indian. He played in the backfield at right half while Thorpe played left half. In 1912, on a Saturday, Carlisle played Army, bidding for national honors. Thorpe played one of his finest games, but his touchdown of twenty-five yards was called back. The hero of the game for Carlisle turned out to be Arcasa, who ran for three touchdowns as Carlisle beat Army 27 to 6.

Alex Arcasa was raised at Orient, north of Barstow and Kettle Falls. He entered Carlisle in 1909 and made the football team. During 1911 and 1912, the Carlisle players established themselves as one of the great teams in the country. In 1911, Carlisle's record was eleven wins and one loss. In 1912, their record was twelve wins, one loss, and one tie. Thorpe was a two-year all-American, and many thought he was the greatest football player of all time. Arcasa, also an all-American, was important to both Thorpe and Carlisle because he could block, receive passes, and run very well when called upon.

We never felt downtrodden or inferior. We knew we could win whatever the odds. After the football games, when we played on the field, we emulated the great plays made during the game by the all-stars. We were excited by thoughts that one day we would be the all-stars.

During my two years at Chemawa, I did not hear a radio or read a newspaper or magazine. News from outside Chemawa did not reach us. I only heard music when I passed the building where the older students were practicing on violins, basses, and the piano. Sometimes, I heard the school band practicing before they played at the athletic contests. Members of certain tribes sang and drummed occasionally, and I enjoyed much of what I heard. Although I appreciated Indian drumming and singing, I was never able to learn it and perform when I was invited to sit around the drum.

I could not speak my own language except for a few words. Our Sin-Aikst dialect was very difficult, and most of the words required guttural sounds for correct pronounciation. There were several students from other tribes at Chemawa who were quite articulate in their own languages. Sometimes I listened to them talk and wished I had their ability. The students used to speak in English, then switch over to their native language. This seemed so easy for them to do.

It was at these moments that I would wonder about the different tribes and the qualities that made each one distinct. I realized that tribes differed not only in language but in customs, music, dances, designs, and even weapons. They also differed in how they prepared and stored away foods and how they met the challenges of everyday life and survival.

During class hours, we were taught basic reading, writing, and arithmetic. There was a course in geography and another in U.S. history. I noticed that the great Indian leaders like Crazy Horse, Chief Joseph, and

Geronimo were not mentioned. All the heroes were white, and they were people like George Washington, Abraham Lincoln, and Thomas Jefferson. General Custer, who was trained at a place called West Point to kill Indians, proved able to defeat only women, children, and elders of the Lakota and Cheyenne. He was considered a hero even in defeat. Crazy Horse and Gall, who were defending their people and homeland against the invaders, were considered savages. I thought white people had strange ways of choosing heroes.

Lewis and Clark were written about and recognized as heroes. Yet the only person in the Lewis and Clark party who knew where they were was Sacajawea, a sixteen-year-old Shoshone with her baby, Baptiste. She was rarely mentioned in any of the books I read. I reflected years later that it was interesting that Lewis and Clark thought they were breaking new ground. They probably were not aware that the nearly invisible trails they followed to reach the West Coast had been well traveled by countless Indians of many tribes. These trails were used continuously for centuries before Lewis and Clark made their trek into the "wilderness." We younger boys conducted our own history courses at our coffee breaks, covering the greatness of Indian leaders, Indian warriors, and Indian ways.

The teachers at Chemawa were good, better than the teachers at Inchelium. They taught white subject matter very well. They were white, and it is understandable that they knew little or nothing about Indians and our side of history. It was not their job to teach us about Indians or Indian ways. It was their job to teach us white ways.

My first training in art came one day when the teacher brought out color crayons, charcoal, watercolors, paintbrushes, and a lot of paper. She experimented with all the media in front of us, then asked us to pick one medium and draw anything we liked. We were encouraged to express ourselves in our own way. All the media were easy for me to handle, and I produced about a half dozen designs before the class ended.

The teacher noticed how easily I worked and suggested I attend the art classes that were reserved for older students. The teacher told the art instructor about me.

The next day, I went to the art class. The instructor introduced me to the class and showed me a color drawing of their next project. The drawing showed mountains and trees with tepees and people in the foreground. The canvas we were going to use was thirty-five feet long and about ten feet high.

I worked on the canvas with the other students. The paint we used was called oil paint. It was good that we worked out of doors because the smell of oil paint and turpentine was strong and disagreeable. I worked almost three weeks on the project, and I could see that the results would be fine to look at. I handled oil easily and enjoyed it the more I worked with it.

After the backdrop was finished, we positioned some fir trees of various sizes at the sides. A few were placed at the front of the canvas to project depth. Three tepees and other Indian accessories were set up near the painted backdrop. We positioned spotlights to highlight the setting. That night, we tested everything, and I was impressed with our completed work. This was my first experience with painting and working on an art project. I did not know it then, but this new experience would lead to a lifetime of work in the visual arts.

The pageant was an annual fall event, and hundreds of non-Indian spectators came at night to view the show. Indian tales and legends were orated while Indians singers and dancers provided backup. The costumes were the best I had ever seen. Our project looked even better with the costumed orators and performers in front of it.

Christmas came, and a few of the students were allowed to go home to their families for about two weeks. When I was not busy in class and thought about Christmas, I began to sense the pain of being homesick. I could also see the pain of homesickness in friends who would not be going home. It was not so much that I missed celebrating Christmas but that this would be the second year when my mother was not with us and our family would be apart. I wondered how Bernard was doing without Luana and me near him. I hoped Brownie would keep him in good company.

When I went outside, I realized it was raining, and I knew that there would be much snow back home at this time of year. Just as I was feeling my worst, the matron came to my room and told me there was a package for me in her office. We went to her office, and I saw the package on the floor. I looked at the handwriting on the package and knew immediately that the package was from my mother.

I could not wait to get to my room to open it. There was a letter inside the box, and I read it. The letter brought me up to date on what was happening back home. My mother wrote that Bernard was lonesome for Luana and me and was always wondering when we were going to come home. She also said that he was growing and in good health. Brownie was doing fine, too. She mentioned that she had sent a present to Luana. At the end of her letter, she gave me her love and wished me a merry Christmas. I realized that I had not given anyone a Christmas present and felt bad about not having any money.

Inside the package was a pair of roller skates, the type that clamps onto your shoes. The next day I took them outside and put them on. After about an hour, I'd learned how to move about without falling. Later, friends of mine asked if I would teach them how to skate. It was not long before a number of us were taking turns skating around the campus. We put so many miles on the skates that within two weeks we had completely worn them out.

At the end of May, during our first year in Chemawa, Luana and I were allowed to go home for the summer. We were thankful that the school year was over. There was excitement and happiness shown by all who were going home for the summer. Everyone was relieved that the past nine months were over. Reunions with family, friends, and homes would be our reward. Many of us felt that we had earned it. Those who were not returning to family and friends watched the rest of us. Their faces showed their happiness for those of us who were going home. But I could feel deep down the loneliness and despair of the students who were remaining at Chemawa.

We boarded a Greyhound bus at Kickback and headed north. Luana and I had not talked since our mother's visit, and we shared our excitement about seeing Bernard and Brownie again. I noticed that Luana had grown and her appearance had changed. I recalled that I had not seen her very much during our first year at Chemawa. We did not talk, but I know we had common feelings about going home.

After our departure, those who remained began their summer routine. They prepared the soil for the planting of crops. The farmlands were tended throughout the summer until harvest time. Alfalfa was planted, watered, and cut in late summer. Pitchforks were used to load wagons, which were pulled by tractors. When the alfalfa, was dry, it was stacked in the large barns. It was a busy time for all, with little time for play.

We changed buses in Spokane and traveled to Colville, where our dad was waiting for us. As the trip progressed, I finally understood Chemawa's location in relation to Inchelium. The bus carried us north, and I viewed the change in scenery, hoping to see sights that were familiar to me.

8 / Chemawa II

My dad and Brownie were waiting for us as we got off the bus. Brownie was beside himself and was barking and running around in circles. He finally came to me, jumping up and planting his forepaws on my chest, and I embraced him. I had not seen Brownie for nine months, and I was anxious to get home and see Bernard, who was being cared for by the Halls.

My dad spit out his snuff, or snoose, and told me to get behind the steering wheel of the Model T. He taught me how to adjust the gas and spark. He cranked the Model T as Brownie jumped onto the right front fender. Luana and I were surprised to see him do this. My dad said that Brownie had learned to do this a few months earlier and preferred to ride there instead of riding in the back bed or front seat of the Model T. We returned to Inchelium by the familiar route we had traveled so often before. The Model T stirred a trail of dust as it found its way over the gravel-covered road. We enjoyed watching Brownie on the right front fender. He seemed to know that he was leading us home. When we passed livestock or domestic fowl near the road, he barked out greetings to them. His bark was never a challenge. He respected and enjoyed the presence of all beings, whether they went on four legs or two.

At the river, I noticed that a new bridge had replaced the old one. As we crossed over, I was surprised at how wide and still the river was. I looked up the river and noticed that Kettle Falls was no longer visible. There was only a large lakelike body of water where the beautiful falls had once roared. The powerful falls and the raging river had been supplanted by a silence and stillness, devoid of life.

Before we reached our one acre of land, we drove up to the Halls' house to get Bernard. We could see him standing in the doorway. He looked thin, and his overalls had patches on both knees. His shoes were worn, and it looked like he needed new ones. Bernard had a big smile on his face. He ran to Luana and me. We took turns hugging him. The three of us were all tears and smiles. Brownie was running in circles, barking and wagging his tail.

We drove to our property, and I noticed a new house standing within twenty feet of the creek. With help from one of his friends, my dad had built an attractive two-room house, with an attic that could be reached by climbing up a ladder in the one bedroom. There was still no running water or electricity, but the house was pleasant inside, and you could open the front door and look out at the creek flowing by.

Bernard had grown. He could talk and move about well, and he kept his balance when he ran. He made it a point to show us all parts of the new house. He told us that the old house was gone. Bernard and Brownie followed Luana and me everywhere. They did not want us out of their sight. Both of them had missed us and were happy that Luana and I were finally home.

After being home for a few days, I decided to go fishing at Hall Creek. I found my old fishing pole and dug some angleworms down by the creek. The trout in the creek were still where I had left them, and they had grown. My walk to Hall Creek began at 9:00 in the morning. Brownie went with me. Hall Creek was about a mile and a half from our house. Brownie and I walked a narrow trail, sheltered by many pine trees, to reach the area I wanted to fish. The creek looked the same, and I checked around the shore and banks for any human signs. When I found none, I went on to fish down the creek in the direction of the Columbia River.

The fishing was good, and as I made my way down the creek, I continued to check for human signs, like footprints, cigarette butts, or discarded fishing gear. As far as I went, nothing could be seen. I was confident that no one had fished the creek since I was last there more than eleven months ago. After fishing for two hours, I decided to take a break. I climbed on top of a large rock, put my pole aside, and sat down to admire the view with Brownie by my side.

I had always admired the blending of mountainous country with large rocks and flowing water. I did not think anything could be more beautiful except when four-legged beings became a part of it. After sitting for a while, Brownie and I walked farther down the creek. We frightened about five grouse. I had not brought my .22 with me, so I just fished for about another hour, then decided to return home. I had caught a dozen trout, and after I cleaned them, Brownie and I climbed to a different trail that would get us home faster. This had been a good day, and I was happy to be home.

I was curious about how the Columbia River had changed, so after breakfast the next day, I decided to walk down to look at it. The walk was about two and a half miles. Brownie went with me, and we took our time looking at old landmarks along the way and reminiscing about things past. I carried my .22 in case I saw a deer or grouse. We finally reached the river, and I studied an area where logging trucks dumped their logs into the river. Hundreds of logs were floating in the river, forming a large raftlike assembly. They were surrounded and held in place by a chain of logs cabled together.

Brownie and I walked about two miles south and looked at the water where Old Inchelium used to be. All the old landmarks were gone, and it looked as if another world had replaced the one I'd grown up in. I could see a new ferry crossing the river, larger and faster than the old one. The beauty of the river, the landmarks, and the area that had once existed were gone. Although it was hard to accept, I realized I would never see them again.

I was ten years old, and I suddenly felt old. I knew my boyhood was behind me and the old ways were gone, never to return. Thoughts of my grandfather, White Grizzly Bear, and other relatives of the past came to me. I imagined I felt the same way they had felt when they lost their homelands, long before my time.

Brownie and I walked away from the river and took another trail that would get us home faster. Thoughts of the past lingered, but I knew I must accept the changes that had come. I was now prepared to put the past aside and face whatever came my way.

During the summer, I did not go far from home. Occasionally, I fished at Hall Creek. I would fish in the morning and then return home so I could spend part of every day with Bernard. Once, I walked to the sub-agency and saw that all the construction work was completed. Lawns were planted, and all the buildings and houses were painted white. The streets were paved, and small trees shaded the sidewalks.

While I was at the agency, I saw Miss Jones, the nurse. She was standing outside the door of her house, looking at her yard. A cigarette was held firmly between her tightly set thin lips. Miss Jones always had a frown on her face that was accented by her arched right eyebrow. She always seemed to be in deep thought. Miss Jones was white, and she was strictly business and to the point, always dressed in her white nurse's uniform and white cap. She had served as a nurse during World War I, caring for wounded soldiers in more than one combat zone. Everyone in Inchelium liked her. Miss Jones was the one who provided minor medical care to those who needed it, while patients with more serious ailments went to the agency hospital in Nespelem, about forty-eight miles away. When it was necessary, she transported people to Nespelem by car. She was honest and sincere with everyone she knew on the reservation. People depended on her and respected her. I guessed her age to be about forty-five years.

Miss Jones saw me and waved me over. She asked if I knew how to mow a lawn, and I told her I had never done it before. She showed me the lawnmower and asked me to try it. It was hard to push, but after a while I got the feel of it, so she offered me a job cutting her grass. I began to mow the lawn, and it took me two hours to complete the job. This included raking the cut grass and putting it into a large burlap sack.

After that, Miss Jones invited me into her kitchen and offered me a glass of water and a bowl of homemade vanilla ice cream. As I was eating, she asked, "Do you enjoy going to school at Chemawa?" I replied that it was a good school, different from the school at Inchelium, and with a lot more buildings and students. "There are many tribes there," I added, "and each one is a little different from ours." She asked what my plans were when I finished school, and I told her I didn't know. She continued, "It is hard here on the reservation. There are never enough jobs. I believe you should think about learning a trade or studying at college if you are able." She told me not to forget what she had told me. Then she gave me $3.00 and said, "Study hard at Chemawa. Try to learn and remember as much as possible. It will help you when you get older. Things have not gotten better here, and I think they will get worse."

I did not know much about college, but I knew that was the place to go for people who wanted to become doctors or lawyers. As the years went by, I never forgot the advice Miss Jones gave me. She was easy to like, and I knew she sometimes picked up my mother when she saw her hitchhiking to Nespelem or Colville.

Some of my friends and relatives were curious about Chemawa and asked me how I liked the school. I told them about the school and answered most of their questions. They did not know where Chemawa was located, so I had to tell them. We all noticed that we had changed and had grown taller and heavier. One day, we went to Twin Lakes and spent the day swimming and boat riding. We also hiked the trails between the two resorts on North Twin.

It was still as beautiful as ever, and many white campers and their families were already at the resorts preparing to enjoy their vacations. I noticed there were always more whites than Indians fishing on Twin Lakes. They were well equipped with shiny new fishing poles and bright dangling lures. This is the type of equipment you need to catch the big rainbow at the lakes.

The summer went by quickly, and it would soon be time to return to Chemawa. We were not able to see our mother because she could not get off work. She now lived farther west, in Tacoma, Washington. She wrote letters to me and sent a birthday present and a card that wished me well.

The day came when my dad said it was time to go. We returned Bernard to our foster grandparents, the Halls. Luana and I said good-bye to him. He sensed that he would not see us for a long time, and I could see the sadness in his eyes. We hugged Bernard and said good-bye as Brownie jumped onto the right front fender of the Model T. My dad, Luana, and I headed, with Brownie, for Colville. We arrived as the bus was loading. I hugged Brownie, said good-bye to my dad, and got on the bus with Luana. It was another sad day because I knew I would not see my family or home again for at least nine months.

Back at Chemawa, we saw several friends as we walked from Kick-back to the campus. Some were picking string beans in the fields along the roadway. A number had stayed at Chemawa for the summer because they had no home other than the school. When I thought about this, I realized that Luana and I were fortunate for what we had. I know our family had problems, but it was worse for some of my friends. They did not complain, and they lived life as it came. At least Chemawa offered lodging, food, and the chance to learn many things for those who set their minds to it.

The sadness of my first year was behind me. Once I entered the campus, I looked forward to learning new things and meeting new students. Those of us who had been in Brewer Hall the year before were happy to know that the old matron was gone. A new matron had replaced her. She was friendly and more considerate. I felt that this year would be better for us. There was no matron's assistant to be concerned about. As time went by, the matron and the boys in Brewer Hall worked together in harmony.

Large numbers of students were coming in every day. I knew most of the boys, but I could see several who were new. It was a repeat of last year, when some arrived wearing moccasins and braided hair. Some hardly spoke at all, as if they did not want to commit anything to anyone.

All of us had to go through the lice shampoo and short haircuts. I had outgrown my old clothes and shoes, so receiving the blue denims was a welcome experience. We were all taught again how to make our beds, march, and brush our teeth. We were also taught once more how to clean and maintain ourselves and our dorms. Those of us who had gone through this before felt like veterans. We enjoyed watching the newcomers struggle to learn a new way of life. The number of students, more than 900, was larger than last year's.

We heard that the football team was going to be better than last year's team. Several of us spent our off-hours watching the team practice after classes. We marveled at the speed of the backfield and the strength and blocking ability of the line. The players seemed bigger this year, and it looked like Chemawa would be hard to beat. All of us were anxious for the season to begin. We all expected a winning season.

I was now in the fifth grade. I had grown taller and heavier during the summer, and my thoughts had changed, too. I was interested in the buildings where the trades were taught. For some reason, I wanted to see these buildings and look inside.

I was intrigued by the equipment the older students were using. I wanted to know how they worked and how they fabricated their specific products. In one building, I saw students making shoes. I realized that these same students, or others who had studied before them, had made the shoes I was wearing. I was impressed that students so young could make such things. I learned later that the clothes I wore were also made by high school students at Chemawa.

Whenever I could, I stood off to one side and watched intently every move the older students made. I was very much interested in the shops where a person could learn to be a carpenter, machinist, blacksmith, welder, and printer. I was too young to study these trades at the time. In later years, my experiences in these trades would help me in my careers of designer, sculptor, and, finally, art director and curator.

Our coffee-drinking rituals resumed in the wooded area. Several boys who were new to Chemawa joined us. Talk of home was always a part of our conversations, and we covered again the great Indian leaders and brave warriors who had fought against the cavalry in the past. We compared battles and then took a vote on who were the greatest leaders and warriors. Crazy Horse and Geronimo always seemed to rate the highest. Chief Joseph and Tecumseh were very close to the top.

We also started to talk about white people. We assumed they were all very rich to be able to afford the houses they lived in and the cars they drove. One day, a Warm Springs said, "They must be very smart to be able to live as they do." "They are rich because of what they have taken from Indians," countered a Spokane. After thinking about this, we decided the Spokane was right. All of us, regardless of tribe, knew that we had traditional enemies, but we agreed that our worst enemy was the white people who had stolen our land and taken what was on and within it.

Our war games did not seem as interesting as they had last year. The boys my age seemed to have changed and matured. We were ready to be a part of something else, but we did not know what it was. Things that appealed to us last year now seemed like child's play, but we were too young to engage in the activities of the older students. We devoted a lot of time to drinking coffee, thinking, and searching for things to do.

As predicted, the new Chemawa football team was better than the old one. Saluskin, Slo-Joe, and LaRocque, the all-stars in the backfield, made great runs. They were hard to stop. It was a great team, with speed and good blocking ability. During the games we saw on our home field, everything came together. We marveled at the plays that always seemed to result in touchdowns.

The victories on the football field made life at Chemawa easier to handle because they diminished any negative feelings we might have had about our situations and ourselves. We all felt that we were a part of a whole. Although we came from many tribes and from different parts of the country, we thought of Chemawa as a tribe. We were confident that we could vanquish all foes and emerge the victor in all wars.

On December 7, late in the day, we were assembled in the entry hallway of the dorm. The matron told us that the Japanese had attacked Pearl Harbor. American ships had been bombed by airplanes, killing many servicemen. She went on to say that we were now at war with Japan.

For reasons I cannot explain, we started to cheer. Afterward, I learned that no one knew who the Japanese were or where Pearl Harbor was. I believe now that we cheered only because we were going to war. It really did not matter who the enemy was. It just seemed important that we were going to war.

From then on, all window blinds had to be drawn at night and lights were turned out early. During the day, the boys in our dorm were assigned to lookout watch for two hours. Two boys shared the duty and were responsible for reporting any planes they saw in the air. When an airplane was seen, the lookouts were to report it immediately to the people in the post office store on the campus.

We used our eyes to search the sky. All of us took our responsibility seriously. We felt this was an important duty, and we allowed nothing to distract us during our two-hour watch. The aircraft watch continued until I finally left Chemawa in May 1942.

Later, during the spring of 1942, I began to see many freight cars loaded with military equipment passing through Chemawa. Uniformed soldiers with helmets and rifles guarded them. It was exciting to see this, and we guessed we were in a very big war.

The end of May had come, and Luana and I were told we would be going home on a train. We learned that our dad had arranged the trip and would meet us at a town called Wilbur, Washington. Luana and I said good-bye to our friends and told them we would see them again in the fall. We boarded the train at the Chemawa railroad station. From our seats, we waved to our friends through the window of the passenger car. This was the first time Luana and I had ever been on a train, and we enjoyed the comfortable conditions and large size. We had never experienced such luxury. Once the train was moving, we marveled at its speed as it traveled north.

Luana and I did not know it then, but this was the last time we would see Chemawa and most of the friends we had made there. Chemawa, a school designed to "civilize" Indians, was to have a lasting impact on my life. I learned things there that I could not have learned anywhere else. My mind and my hands were taught skills that would later help me excel in two professions that I did not even expect to enter.

Chemawa may have succeeded in "civilizing" me, but it did not separate me from the Indian culture. It did the opposite. Chemawa introduced me to my culture. It did this by enabling me to meet and get to know several Indian boys my age. These boys knew their cultures and were gracious enough to share their knowledge with me. Fortunately for me, the boys came from different tribes. This enabled me to learn, appreciate, and differentiate between several Indian cultures. It would have been impossible to do this back home in Inchelium.

The knowledge I gained in Chemawa stimulated me to learn more about the total Indian culture. I continue to do this today. When I visit bookstores, I automatically review any new books about Indians. Newspaper and magazine articles about Indians are read and reread.

The train made its way north to Portland through some small towns, then headed east through the beautiful country along the Columbia River, which separates Oregon from Washington. As we traveled through the Gorge, I saw a number of waterfalls that reminded me of Kettle Falls. Near one, I saw a few Indians and wondered which falls I was seeing. I learned later that it was Celilo Falls. A number of tribes that lived along the Columbia River, including the Yakima and Umatilla Indians, harvested their salmon at these falls. After passing the Gorge, the train headed northeast, passed through miles of arid terrain, and arrived at last at Spokane, Washington.

We changed trains at Spokane and boarded a smaller one, which traveled west through more small towns in very dry country. Rock-terraced terrain with numerous pine trees began to appear. I appreciated the familiar smell of the trees and land as we approached Wilbur. I sensed that we were getting close to our homeland and looked forward to arriving there with growing excitement.

My dad and Bernard were standing by the Model T waiting for us. It was good to see them again. Bernard had grown and had a big grin on his face. He began to show off by exhibiting how far he could throw rocks. He was obviously happy that Luana and I were home. I noticed that Brownie was missing and asked, "Where is Brownie?" My dad spit out his snoose and answered, "We left him at our camp to watch over things. You will see him soon. He is OK." My dad had to buy some food and other necessities, so we went into downtown Wilbur for about an hour. I noticed that there was a movie theater in town and hoped that we would return one day to see a movie.

9 / Manila Creek

The Model T never seemed to change. It had its usual coat of dust, and the motor sounded good as we cruised at a speed of about 25–30 miles per hour. My dad told Luana and me that we were going to live in the Keller area of the reservation, where the Sanpoil River drains into the Columbia River. He said he was working for a logging outfit as a brush piler in the Manila Creek area up in the mountains.

As we traveled, Bernard told us that he and my dad lived in a tent by a creek. He added that there were a lot of big trees. Bernard said there were many animals, birds, and rattlesnakes. He said that rattlesnakes were very dangerous. He told us we must be very careful where we walked because a bite could kill us.

We finally left the wheat fields surrounding Wilbur. The Model T descended a winding grade with a beautiful view of the Columbia River. Before we reached the bottom of the grade, we stopped at a spring that gushed from the mountainside. My dad told us that this was the coldest water in the area. We cupped the water in our hands and drank. It was the coldest and sweetest water I had ever tasted. We continued our descent and saw a ferry waiting below. The river was very wide at this point, and I remembered the smell and feel of the river as the ferry carried us across. When we reached the opposite shore, we were back on the Colville Indian Reservation.

We headed north and then west up into the mountains to reach Manila Creek. About a mile off the main road, we came to our new home, a makeshift tent my dad had constructed by tying together various pieces of canvas. The tent was alongside a small creek and was surrounded by pine and fir trees. A rock-covered hill stood on the other side of the dirt road.

We saw Brownie tied to a tree, and he was overjoyed to see Luana and me. I untied him, and we began to play. I picked up a stick and threw it, and Brownie ran to retrieve it as he always had, with his tail wagging from side to side. We unloaded the supplies my dad had bought in Wilbur and carried them into the tent. Upon entering the tent, Bernard showed me the sleeping area my dad had made by cutting pine and fir boughs and placing them on the ground. Burlap bags covered the boughs, and blankets lay on top of the burlap bags.

In the opposite corner of the tent was a homemade stove that had been cut with a steel chisel from the end of a large steel drum. The flat end was up to provide a cooking surface. Wood could be inserted through a square opening cut out of the side, and a hole at the end of the drum held a stovepipe that carried smoke out of the tent area. My dad had even installed a damper in the stovepipe to control the heat.

My dad warned us that this was rattlesnake country and said that we should always be careful. He raised the blankets and the burlap bags to make sure no rattlesnakes had crawled under them to sleep or escape the hot sun. He told us to always do this before lying down or playing in the sleeping area.

A gasoline lamp provided light when it became dark. We could raise a flap on the side of the tent to let in fresh air if it got too warm at night. After eighteen months at Chemawa, with electric lights, running water, indoor plumbing, and a central heating system, we were now back to living in canvas shelters that had been put together by my dad. We were reminded of our earlier way of life. Once again, we would be living out of doors close to the other beings and in harmony with our environment.

On our first night in our new home, we were engulfed in the aroma of pine and fir boughs. We could hear an owl announcing its presence nearby and the choruses of coyotes in the distance. I listened to the wind blowing through the treetops above and talked to it softly. I thanked the Great Spirit for keeping our family well and protecting Bernard and Brownie. I thanked the Great Spirit for allowing us to live together again. It was good to be back on the reservation, and I was anxious to explore my surroundings when morning came. We drifted into sleep to the sounds of the small creek flowing by and the songs of many crickets.

After breakfast the next morning, my dad told me that he had to go to work and I could help him. He showed me a small double-bladed ax he had bought for me. It was used and rusty but still in good condition. My dad handed me my old .22 Stevens and a box of shells. He said there were many grouse in the area and I might be able to get a few for dinner. Before we left, he instructed Luana to watch and take care of Bernard while we were working. He warned Luana again about rattlesnakes and told her to be careful where she and Bernard walked. He said it would be wise to keep Brownie close by because the dog knew how to handle them.

I followed my dad along a logging road and we went farther up into the mountains. There were several quail along the way. They quickly flew out of harm's way as we approached. I had never seen quail in Inchelium, and they seemed too small to shoot for food. After we had walked about a mile and a half, we reached the area where a large number of trees had been felled by four fallers who worked with the logging outfit.

My dad took my ax and swung it so that it stuck into a stump. He produced a file and showed me how to file in one direction, away from me, along the blade of the ax. He gave me the file, and after a few tries, I knew how to sharpen the blade of an ax. My dad then sharpened his ax, which was larger than mine. After he finished, he told me we had to chop the limbs off all the fallen trees and place them in piles.

We started work at 8:00 in the morning and continued to chop limbs and place them in piles until noon. We took a break to drink water and eat the peanut-butter-and-honey sandwiches my dad had prepared. He said we would rest for one hour. Since I had about a half hour to kill, I picked up my .22 and decided to look for some grouse. I hunted along a hillside but saw nothing except a few squirrels, several chipmunks, and a rabbit, so I returned to the work site and went back to work.

It was getting hot. We perspired heavily and had to drink a lot of water from the water bag. My dad spit out his snoose and washed out his mouth with water. He told me that the brush piles would be burned in the early winter, when they would not start any forest fires. We worked until 5:00 in the afternoon, then went back to our campsite.

While my dad and I worked, Luana and Bernard discovered that the pinecones the squirrels were carrying up into the trees were full of tasty little nuts. So they gathered pinecones, removed the nuts, and put the nuts into a bowl. The nuts were small, and it took a long time to gather any amount, but the results were worth the effort. The nuts were very tasty. We stored them away, and when we got hungry between meals, we had the pine nuts for snacks. Luana also devoted time to teaching Bernard about numbers and the ABCs. She wanted to prepare him for school the following year. Luana taught Bernard in the same manner that our mother had taught us years earlier. Bernard became an avid learner, and he and Luana grew very close during that summer.

Work was continuous throughout the summer, and the weather got very hot. My dad was right. There were many rattlesnakes in the Manila Creek area. I killed several in the areas where we worked. Once, after work, while Luana and I were getting water at the creek, we saw a large one, about three feet long. While she dipped the jug into the creek to fill it, the snake crawled to safety in the brush beside the creek.

One Saturday, I decided to go hunting. Brownie came with me. We walked to a small valley with many trees. I decided to follow a deer trail along the hillside, hoping to see a deer. As I was walking, I heard Brownie growling and barking behind me. I could also hear hissing and the sounds I thought would come from the rattles of a rattlesnake. I turned around and saw that he had cornered what looked like a very large rattlesnake, but when I got closer, I realized it was a bull snake. The bull snake was trying to frighten Brownie off by pretending it was a rattlesnake. I studied the snake for awhile. I had heard that bull snakes killed and ate rattlesnakes. Sensing that we would not hurt it, the bull snake uncoiled and crawled away. I called for Brownie, and we continued to hunt.

There were many grouse, and they were easy to hit with my .22, so we had grouse for dinner often during the summer. When we took a day off on Sundays, I would walk down to Manila Creek and fish. There were many mountain trout, but they were not as large as the ones in Hall Creek. I could tell by human signs along the creek that others fished there, so I did not expect to find large trout.

On other Sundays, when we were not working, we went down to the small town of Keller, which consisted of only one store. The Sanpoil River entered the Columbia close to Keller, so we would spend part of the day fishing off the banks of the Sanpoil. This part of the reservation was very beautiful. Salmon once went up this river to spawn in large numbers before Grand Coulee Dam ended all salmon runs. The Sanpoil Indians in Keller still celebrate their "Salmon Days." At this get-together, they pay tribute to the salmon of the past.

The only fish we caught in the Sanpoil were small perch, crappie, and carp. Perch were small, about seven to eight inches long, but they were tasty when fried. The crappie were edible, but the carp were large, fat, and heavy, and no one ate them. We always threw them back into the water to live another day.

During the summer, my dad wrote a letter to Judge Brown in Okanogan. He requested that Luana and I be allowed to stay in the Keller area and attend school there in the fall. My dad informed Judge Brown that he had steady work in the woods and could afford to have Luana and me live with him. He also stated that the Keller School was a good one. After a few weeks, a letter arrived from Judge Brown granting my dad permission to keep us in Keller.

At this point, I realized that Luana and I had probably seen the last of Chemawa, and I had both good and bad thoughts about staying in Keller. The good part was that we could help take care of Bernard and Brownie; the bad part was that we would probably never see our friends again.

I also thought about the trade schools I had hoped to attend one day. I knew I would not be able to work with the equipment in the trade schools now. I would also miss seeing the all-stars playing football, basketball, and track.

One day, a boy about my age drove by our camp area in an old International Truck. The truck was a little smaller than a logging truck and had a flatbed with no side rails or back. It seemed unusual that a boy so young should be driving a truck that large. About fifteen minutes later, he approached our camp area going in the opposite direction, stopped, and got out of the truck.

The boy walked up to where I was sitting. He was thin, with disheveled hair, light skin, and freckles across his nose. He was about two inches taller than I was. I judged him to be a half-breed.

The boy said, "My name is Benny. What's yours?" "Lawney," I answered. Benny asked where I was from, and I told him that I used to live in Inchelium but had spent the last two years in Chemawa. He said he'd never heard of Chemawa, and I told him that Chemawa was in Oregon. "Only Indians go there," I explained. "I'm an Indian," he remarked, and I asked what kind of Indian he was. When he answered that he was part Sanpoil, I told him I was a Lake. Benny asked if I wanted to go for a ride in his truck, and I nodded yes.

Benny drove his International over most of the logging roads. He was a very good driver and handled the truck with ease. He told me that his name was Benny Aubertin and that he lived with his brother Dick and his dad and mother near George Whitelaw's home. George Whitelaw had a logging outfit and logged near the same area where my dad worked.

I was impressed with how well Benny drove his truck. When he told me he was nine years old, I was even more impressed. One day, while we were riding up the logging roads, Benny asked me if I knew how to drive. I told him that my dad was teaching me but I had a lot to learn. He offered to teach me how to drive his International, and I accepted with a nod. I was unsure of myself because the truck was large and the controls were very different from the Model T's.

Benny taught me how to shift the gears and work the clutch. Learning to drive the International was difficult at first and a lot different from driving the Model T. But after several tries, I got the feel of it. I soon learned to stop the truck smoothly without killing the motor.

When Benny got behind the steering wheel, he said, "Watch how I do this." He stepped on the clutch and shifted to a lower gear. He stepped on the clutch again and shifted another gear lower. He told me, "This is how you double-clutch, to slow the truck down without using your brakes." This impressed me and I was anxious to try it myself. Benny patiently taught me how to downshift, and by day's end, I knew how to double-clutch the International.

One day, while we were driving the roads of Manila Creek, I mentioned that there were sure a lot of rattlesnakes here, but there were no rattlesnakes in Inchelium. Benny asked why we didn't have them there, and I told him I didn't know. "There are no quail there either," I added.

"Well, we have a lot of rattlesnakes and quail here," Benny said. "There are even more along the Sanpoil River. There are rainbow in the river, and fishermen like to fish there. You have to be careful because of the rattlers. One time, a dog was bitten and he almost died." He pulled to the side of the road to let a logging truck go by. It was loaded with logs, and as the truck passed, the driver waved. "There used to be a lot of salmon in the Sanpoil, but they are all gone now," Benny went on. He shook his head, "We only have perch, crappie, and carp. Some people eat perch, but hardly anyone cares for crappie. The carp are big and ugly, and no one eats them. When you hook into them, they don't put up a fight. It's like reeling in a dead log."

I agreed with what Benny had said and told him that we didn't have any salmon either. "Our people used to catch them at Kettle Falls, but it is flooded over now. No one catches anything." I told Benny, "The Columbia River used to be beautiful. I enjoyed being near it. I liked to swim in the river. It used to be so clean."

Benny nodded. "I remember that. It was that way here where the Sanpoil enters the Columbia. It was good then. The river is dead now."

As we came to a curve in the road, Benny shifted to a lower gear. "The People don't have much food now," he said. "We eat a lot more deer. When we can't find the deer, times really get hard. There is never enough to eat. My dad works with a logging outfit. If it were not for that, we would be in bad shape. The only work here is logging. That is the only thing that brings in any money. Those who have ranches barely make it. I don't know how people without ranches make it at all."

"They must eat a lot of grouse and mountain trout," I answered, then added, "that's what our family depends on. We live mostly on what I can shoot or catch with my fishing pole."

Benny nodded, "That is how we make it, also."

Later, we saw Benny's brother, Dick, and although he was only a few years older than I was, he was almost six feet tall. I found out that he was very good at playing baseball and adept at pitching. When we stood beside him, he towered head and shoulders above us. We became friends, and the three of us spent many days fishing, hunting, and exploring the Manila Creek area.

One day, just before quitting time, a faller cut a tree that landed on a porcupine. The faller had to kill the porcupine to keep it from suffering. My dad and I studied the dead porcupine. I was curious about the quills that projected from its body. They were needle sharp, and I remembered the decorative quillwork on the Indian vests I had seen at Chemawa. I wondered how the Indians colored the quills and bent them into shapes to make beautiful designs on vests, moccasins, and other attire.

When my dad realized that the faller was not going to take the porcupine, he asked if he could have it. The faller seemed surprised and answered, "You can have it if you want it, Julian. What are you going to do with it?" My dad said, "I'm going to take it home and cook it." The faller looked more surprised and laughed. He asked, "Have you ever eaten a porcupine?" My dad spit out his snoose and answered, "No, but it should be okay once it is cooked. Come over to our camp in a couple of hours and join us for dinner." The faller grinned and shook his head.

My dad tied a piece of rope around the porcupine's hind leg and wrapped a piece of canvas around the body so the quills would not poke him as he carried it. When we reached our camp, my dad skinned the porcupine and removed its insides. Then he butchered it and put the pieces in a large pot and added water to it.

He started a fire in the stove and started to cook the porcupine. While the porcupine was cooking, my dad prepared some rice and vegetables to go with it. After about two hours, he said that supper was ready. Luana filled a plate for Bernard, then a plate for herself. I did the same for myself. We had no table, so we sat on a grass-covered area away from the dust. Luana and I tried to eat the porcupine, but the taste was too strong. My dad and Bernard were not deterred and managed to eat large portions that night. After three more meals, they had completely eaten the porcupine.

We discovered that a family lived about a mile away and had a cow, pigs, and some chickens. The family was white but seemed friendly. One day, my dad asked if they had any milk for sale. The man who owned the small farm nodded and we were able to have fresh milk. We also purchased eggs. We kept the milk cold by pouring it into a large jar and placing the jar in the small creek.

Immersing food in the creek preserved perishable food during the hot weather. We put food in mason jars and secured the lids so flies and other insects could not get in. The jars were placed in the water along the shaded banks of the creek.

We had to be careful when we were near the creek because of the rattlesnakes. There were so many around our campsite that it was not wise to walk around at night. There was always the possibility we might step on one. We were constantly aware of this and were careful about where we walked. Brownie was also careful at night and stayed close to our canvas shelter. He slept at the entrance to our shelter to make sure no rattlers crawled in while we slept.

The summer had ended, and the weather was getting colder. Because we needed more fuel for the stove, Luana and Bernard gathered the dead limbs of trees and dragged them close to our tent. I chopped them with my ax to make firewood for the stove, and Luana and Bernard piled the wood next to the tent.

By the end of October, we knew it would soon be too cold to live in the tent. We searched the Manila Creek area for a house. After driving the roads in the area, we realized that the only vacant house was a deserted one about a mile from where we were camped. We had seen the house several times before and never thought we would have to live in it. It had been deserted for years and was in poor condition. But we had no choice, so we went in and cleaned it out.

The house was built of lumber, and in half a dozen places the knots had fallen out, leaving holes in the walls. It had two windows, which were still intact although one was cracked. The floor was made of lumber with knots missing in a few places, and we could see where mice had come in by the messes they had left here and there. The shed-type roof was covered with old tar paper, which still managed to keep the inside of the house dry. The door was sagging at the hinges, had no lock, and needed repair, but it was still usable. There were no interior walls, and the two-by-four framework was exposed, studded with rusty nails driven in at random for hanging up objects. A hundred feet from the house stood an old outhouse, still sturdy enough to be used. Pine trees and a few firs surrounded the house. The house, I thought, fit the site well.

We found some old boards and made platforms to sleep on and a table for eating and studying. Two old apple boxes, reinforced with new nails, became our chairs. We saved the lids from canned food and nailed them on top of the knotholes in the floor and walls. There was a stove near the corner of the room. The stove was oblong in shape and flat on top. It was designed to throw heat as well and was ideal for our needs. The stove was very dirty, and we spent a lot of time cleaning it before we could build a fire in it to test it. When we finally did, we found that it worked fine. A gasoline lamp and two kerosene lamps provided our light.

We used a porcelain-faced metal basin for daily washing, and the large metal tub where we cleaned our clothes also served for our baths. When we bathed, we hung up a blanket for privacy. The tub was heavy when it was filled, and Luana had to help me carry it out to empty the used water. My dad always bathed in the nearby creek. He continued to do this even when it got so cold that ice formed on the creek banks. The house was about 200 feet from the creek. We had all the water we needed. About three weeks after we moved in, the first snow fell, but we were ready for it, and the stove threw out enough heat to keep the chill out. The house had only one room, but it provided about eight times as much space as the tent.

When school started, a car came to pick us up every morning and brought us back after school. The road up to Manila Creek was hard to maneuver on when the snow fell. The car needed chains to get anywhere. Even then, it sometimes got stuck, and we arrived late for school or were late getting home. Six other students our age lived in the Manila Creek area. Two were white, the children of ranchers who had cut out the acres they farmed from the surrounding forest. The other four were Indians, Dick, Benny, and two others from the Rickard family. Since Bernard was too young to go to school, my dad found an elderly couple who lived nearby. They agreed to take care of Bernard while my dad worked.

The school at Keller was about seven miles from where we lived. There were two classrooms in the school and four grades in each room. Teaching that many grades was difficult, but the teachers did a good job. Classes went along smoothly, and the students seemed to appreciate their teachers' efforts. About a third of the students were white, but everyone seemed to know everyone else, and we all got along fine.

In addition to teaching the regular classes, the teachers kept us abreast of what was happening in the war. They displayed large maps and pointed out the various countries that were directly involved in the war. I was surprised to see how small Germany and Japan were. I could not see how they thought they could win against a country as big as the United States. The teachers also told us that the leaders of Germany and Japan were Hitler and Tojo. They said that Mussolini was the leader of Italy.

Occasionally, we saw young men of the tribe in uniforms. Most were in the army, but some were in the navy and the marines. They were home on leave. Many expected to see action in the near future. I thought they were the best-dressed Indians on the reservation. I noticed they were the only ones who had short hair and polished shoes.

We used a battery-powered radio to receive news and entertainment. Most of the news seemed to be about the war, and as the weeks went by, I became very much interested in it. At night, after studying and before going to sleep, we also listened to programs like *I Love a Mystery* and shows featuring such popular radio personalities as Charlie McCarthy and Fibber Magee and Molly. I enjoyed hearing what I found out later was classical music. I had heard this music on the radio sometimes when I was in Inchelium. I had not known what the music was about, but I had liked it. Now I began to appreciate its beauty and power. I had no idea who had written the music or where it came from, but I sensed that it was very special. Years later, I learned that Beethoven, Tchaikovsky, Puccini, and Bizet had composed my favorites.

Sometimes, my dad practiced his guitar. He taught me a few fingering positions, and after awhile, I learned how to strum simple chords. I finally got good enough to accompany him as he played the lead on another guitar. He was very good on the guitar. His fingers were heavily calloused and no longer limber, but he still produced good music. Occasionally, he gave guitar lessons on his own time to earn extra money. My dad told me that before he met my mother, he used to sell guitars for Lana Turner's dad, who ran a music store in Wallace, Idaho.

Sometimes the loggers who worked with my dad dropped by to listen to him play. I accompanied him when I knew the songs. The loggers seemed to enjoy the music we produced. As my dad and I played, the loggers drank whiskey straight from the bottle, smoked cigarettes, and continually tapped or stomped their feet to our music. The only times they did not move their feet was when my dad played his favorite songs. One was called "When I Grow Too Old to Dream." The other was "The Story of the Glory of Love," which contained the words "You have to give a little, take a little, let your poor heart break a little." There was always quiet from the loggers when my dad played and sang these songs. But when we played the fast and lively "Double Eagle," the loggers clapped their hands, drank whiskey from the bottle, and stomped their feet.

During the winter months, our food supplies began to run low. My dad was unable to work much because of heavy snowfall and very cold weather. One day, three loggers asked my dad to join them in a deer hunt.

They left early in the morning and did not return until nightfall. My dad was not lucky and did not even fire his 32.40, but two of the others got a deer apiece. They gave us a hind leg, which helped us get through part of the winter. I could not find any grouse. We had to ration what food we had. I caught trout in the creek now and then, and this helped put food on the table until the weather broke and warmer days came.

When spring came, I planted a garden under the supervision of my dad. I spent many hours preparing the soil and then keeping the garden clear of weeds. Luana and Bernard helped me. I dug a ditch from the creek to my garden so I could irrigate my plants regularly. All the work and attention pay off, and during the summer we would have fresh vegetables to add to our food supply.

One day in June 1943, my dad was helping me prepare my fishing line. He was attaching a new spinner and a few sinkers. It was about 4:30 in the afternoon. We were sitting on the one-step porch outside our front door when my dad accidentally dropped a sinker through a crack in the step. He slipped his left hand behind the step to retrieve it and felt something prick the back of his hand. He looked at his hand and decided he had been poked by the pine needles that lay scattered all over the place.

After a few minutes, my dad checked his hand again and saw that it was beginning to swell. He looked closer and observed, "I think a snake bit me." I inspected his hand and noticed two small holes where a little blood was starting to flow. My dad removed the pipe from his mouth and remarked, "There must be a snake under the porch."

I asked my dad if he wanted me to pull the porch loose, and he nodded. I pried the porch away from the house with the handle of a shovel. I yelled, "There it is!" A small seven-button rattlesnake lay coiled in the area covered by the porch. My dad said he would be okay if we killed the snake before it reached water. He took his can of snoose from his left shirt pocket, removed the lid, and put a pinch behind his bottom lip. I got the shovel and killed the snake.

Within an hour, my dad's arm was very swollen. We made a sling by ripping an old towel lengthwise and tying the two pieces together so it was long enough to go around his neck. This helped support the weight of his arm, because he was having a hard time moving it.

As my dad's arm kept swelling, I became curious about the rattlesnake. My dad and I had killed several while we worked in the woods, but we'd paid little attention to them. I went to the bushes where I had thrown the snake and studied it. I found two small sticks and pried the mouth open and looked at the two small fangs. My dad looked at the snake with me and said, "Poison runs through the fangs. That is what makes my arm and hand swell." As I looked closely at the fangs, I could see the hollow passages where the poison flowed. I asked my dad where the poison comes from, and he answered, "There are poison sacs in the head of the rattler. That's where it comes from. It doesn't take much to make you sick or kill you." I showed the snake's fangs to Luana and Bernard and explained what my dad had told me. Bernard, as young as he was, showed much interest and seemed to understand everything I told him.

Two loggers who worked with my dad happened to be going by. They stopped and looked at my dad's arm and told him he should get to a doctor right away. My dad replied, "I will be okay if I take some medicine. If it gets worse, I'll go tomorrow."

The nearest doctor was in Wilbur, about twenty-four miles away. The distance was short in miles, but because of the long steep grade, it took the Model T a long time to get there. My dad told me that he would be okay in the morning if he took some medicine. He did not think the bite was serious enough to make the trip to Wilbur. He asked me to rub some liniment on the bite, and I applied it about six times every half hour. He opened a bottle of whiskey and took a big drink from the bottle. He told me that would help kill the poison and continued to drink late into the night. I could hear him moaning through the night and into the early morning until I finally fell asleep.

At 7:00 in the morning, my dad awakened me. He told me, "I guess we had better see a doctor." He continued, "We should try to leave within the hour." I noticed that his swollen left arm was almost twice the size of his right arm. "Does it hurt?" I asked him. He said that it was just heavy and hard to move. The whiskey bottle, which had been full, was almost half empty.

Luana awakened Bernard, washed his face, and helped him put on his clothes. I could tell they were concerned but unaware of the seriousness of the rattlesnake bite. The three of us climbed into the Model T. My dad, his arm in the sling, cranked the Model T to get the motor running. I sat in the driver's seat and adjusted the gas and spark as the motor started.

Because I was twelve years old, I was not allowed to drive, so I moved over to let my dad in behind the steering wheel. It was difficult for him to maneuver the Model T with one arm. When we got onto the ferry, the operator went faster than usual. He wanted to get us across the Columbia quickly. The Model T labored as we climbed the grade, and we had to stop at the spring to get water for the overheated radiator. It took about a gallon of water to cool it. We finally reached the summit. We traveled as fast as we could through the wheat fields to reach Wilbur.

It was 10:00 in the morning when we arrived, and we asked some people where a doctor could be found. The doctor's office was on a side street. We entered the office. The doctor immediately took my dad into the back room. He proceeded to lance the wound by making cuts through the fang marks. Then he injected serum into my dad's arm with an instrument that had a sharp needle. The doctor shook his head. He told my dad it was very late to be doing this and he hoped it would still help. He said time would tell and advised my dad to go home and get as much rest as possible. When he found out where we lived, he shook his head again. He made a new sling for my dad. As we left, he wished my dad good luck.

My dad did not express any real concern in spite of the fact that his swollen arm was twice the size of his good arm. After we left the doctor's office, he reached into his shirt pocket and pulled out his can of snoose. He asked me to open it. I removed the lid with a twist. I read the word "Copenhagen" on the side of the can. My dad reached in with his thumb and forefinger and took out a pinch. He placed it behind his lower lip. I put back the lid and handed him the can, and he returned it to his shirt pocket. He spit at the side of the curb and said that we might as well buy some supplies, like gas for the lamp and bread, peanut butter, and potatoes. An hour later, after he had bought ice cream cones for Luana, Bernard, and me, we were on our way back to Manila Creek.

A logger dropped by a few days later. He pulled a small newspaper clipping from his shirt pocket and remarked, "Julian, you made the papers." There was a small article about my dad's ordeal. I realized then how serious my dad's situation had been.

The logger asked my dad to play some music on his guitar. My dad laughed and asked if he would rather have a drink and some snoose instead. The logger accepted both. He knew how to chew snoose and drink whiskey just like my dad. He took the snoose from the little round can and pushed it into the cheek of his mouth and took a big drink of whiskey from the bottle. The logger looked at my dad's arm and said, "Boy, that arm is really big. How does it feel?" My dad answered, "I can't move my arm, and I can barely move my fingers. But it will be better soon. Probably in a few weeks."

My dad was off work for about five weeks, and during that time he decided to move back to the Inchelium area when he recovered. The Lincoln Lumber Company was assembling a large work force in the upper Hall Creek area near Inchelium. There was a large amount of timber to be cut, and the company was clearing an area and setting up cabins for the loggers and their families. A cookhouse was also being constructed where the loggers could eat, especially the single ones.

The swelling on my dad's arm gradually went down. While he was recovering, he worked on simple chores with his good arm. One day, I helped him repair the brakes of the Model T. I held the metal band while my dad removed the worn brake lining. He put in a new lining and secured it by hammering the brass rivets into place. Other times he worked in the garden. He spent hours weeding the garden and irrigating it when the sun was setting. Luana and Bernard helped my dad and followed all his suggestions. Throughout the summer months, we had a wide variety of fresh vegetables.

My dad wanted to go to Spokane before we left for Inchelium. He wanted to buy parts for the Model T that he could not find in the smaller towns. Early one morning in July, we left for Spokane. We took Brownie on this trip because we knew we would be gone for a few days. Brownie jumped onto the right front fender as my dad and I loaded the Model T with food and extra clothes. My dad tied a five-gallon water tank made of galvanized metal onto the left running board where it joins the left rear fender. The water tank was very handy in hot weather because it had a faucet built into the bottom side, which made it easy to get water for drinking. My dad also filled a water bag and hung it on the hand-crank insert bracket of the Model T. He told us that the air blowing on it as we traveled would keep it cool. I sat in the driver's seat to adjust the gas and spark as my dad cranked the Model T.

We headed for Wilbur. We passed the spring gushing from the mountainside as the Model T labored to the top of the beautiful grade. We turned east in the direction of Davenport. The day grew very hot, and just before we reached Davenport, we had a flat tire. We seemed to have a flat tire every time we took a long trip in the Model T. Luckily, we were near some trees, so we were shaded from the hot sun. Luana and Bernard sat in the shade and played together. Because they had no toys, they amused themselves with things left by nature while my dad and I fixed the tire.

First, I helped my dad jack up the Model T, and he showed me how to unscrew the lug nuts that held the wheel. Once we got the wheel off, he removed the tire from the rim. This had to be done carefully so that you did not pinch the inner tube that contained the air inside the tire. When my dad got the inner tube clear of the tire, he pumped the tube full of air, then listened as he rotated the tube close to his ear. When he heard air escaping from the tube, he marked the hole with a stick of white chalk. I got the tire-patching equipment from the back of the Model T. My dad began to rub around the hole with a rough perforated scraper. He used sandpaper to clean around the hole and applied adhesive to the area. After allowing it to sit for a minute, he lit a match and set the adhesive on fire. About two seconds later, he blew out the flame and immediately put a rubber patch on the hole. He pressed it and held it in place until he was satisfied it was dry.

With the hole patched, my dad pushed the tube into the tire and mounted the tire to the rim. When it fit perfectly, he had me pump the tire full of air. We placed the wheel back onto the wheelbase and screwed it into place with the lug nuts.

As my dad and I worked, Bernard came over and asked questions. He was curious about how we were repairing the Model T and asked several times if he could help. Bernard was fascinated with the car and walked around to study all its different parts. When my dad and I repaired the flat tire and fastened the wheel to the wheelbase, Bernard thought that was a great accomplishment.

We decided to eat before continuing on to Spokane. We brought peanut-butter-and-honey and tuna sandwiches out of the back of the car and ate in the shade of the trees. We finished our lunch with water from the tank. Brownie did not care for peanut butter and honey, but he appreciated half of a tuna sandwich and a bowl of water.

We arrived in Spokane at 4:30 in the afternoon and drove through the busy streets to my dad's favorite hotel. I learned later that it was located in the poorer section of town, close to the Spokane River. All the buildings in the area were old. Day and night, hundreds of people could be seen walking the streets, eating in restaurants, or going in and out of stores and taverns. Sometimes we saw people who were drunk sitting or lying in the alleys drinking wine or whiskey.

We received a lot of attention from the people on the sidewalks when Brownie barked out greetings to our new neighbors as we drove past. When I think back on this now, I'm sure we must have been something to see, riding in our 1923 Model T—dark eyes in three dusty bronze faces peering in wonder at everything before them, and the car, covered with dust from the reservation, its appearance enhanced by Brownie on the right front fender, the five-gallon water tank tied to the rear of the left running board, and the water bag hanging from the hand-crank insert bracket. The engine made a sound that was different from the sounds of other cars, like an old gas-powered lawn mower that was not in tune. It sputtered continually. Sometimes it let out a gasping noise, as if it were fighting to stay alive, which was accented by occasional backfiring. When my dad honked the horn, everybody looked.

We drove to the small parking lot behind the hotel and tied Brownie to the wheel of the Model T with a rope. The rope was long enough so that he could crawl under the car and go to sleep. Water in a large bowl and some bones to chew on were left within reach. Brownie was no trouble at all on long trips. He had an easy disposition and took life in stride. He was a lot like my dad, good-natured and even-tempered. Brownie enjoyed new adventures and knew how to take life as it came.

We went into the hotel, and my dad got a room on the second floor. We could see Brownie and the Model T from our room. Brownie was content, chewing on one of the bones we had left him. Our room had a sink and water for washing or drinking, but the toilet was located down the hall and was shared with others. My dad took us to a restaurant nearby where we each had a bowl of soup and some milk. When we finished eating, he took us for a walk around the city. We enjoyed looking into the windows of all the stores. We saw many things to buy for those who had enough money.

We looked at the movie theaters to see what was playing. There were three theaters in the area. We chose the one that was showing a murder mystery. My dad bought popcorn, and the four of us sat close to the screen.

When the movie was over, we left that theater and went to see another movie about cowboys and Indians. As I watched, the Indians reminded me of Crazy Horse and other Great Plains warriors. I admired the way they rode their horses without using saddles or bridles. I knew the warriors could guide their horses with nothing more than knee pressure. I knew that each one could fire a rifle and release an arrow from a bow with accuracy while riding at a full gallop. I had heard at Chemawa that the Comanche were the best riders on the Plains. The abilities of the Plains Indians impressed me. But in the movie, although the Indians put up a good fight, the cowboys won. I left the theater disappointed.

After the second movie, we took Brownie the leftovers my dad had brought from the restaurant. It was past midnight, so we went to the hotel to go to sleep. It was very hot in the hotel, and we had a hard time sleeping because we could hear drunks talking and walking down the hallways all night long. I thought it might be cooler by the window, and Luana helped me move the bed up to the window so I could hang my feet out into the open air.

The next day was beautiful. After I ate breakfast, I went out to visit Brownie and fed him some leftovers. I filled his bowl with water from the water tank and untied him so he could run around and explore the alley. Meanwhile, my dad went to a garage and found the auto parts he needed. He put them in the back of the Model T.

My dad told us we were going to the Natatorium Park, so we got into the Model T and drove for a couple of miles. Along the way, we saw the

Spokane River, and I wondered if it was good for fishing. We arrived at the park and were delighted at the sight of all the rides. Bernard was fascinated. He had never seen anything like this before. He ran about the grounds with wide eyes, inspecting everything. I recognized the Ferris wheel, a merry-go-round, and bumper cars, among many other rides. There were places selling hamburgers, hot dogs, popcorn, ice cream, and sugar candy—even one with all sorts of soda pop.

There were many people there, all having a good time. The last time I had seen anything like this I had been at the state fair in Salem, Oregon, about two years ago when I was at Chemawa. The Natatorium Park was located right beside the Spokane River. I thought it was a beautiful area. People considered the Natatorium the most popular amusement park in the Inland Empire. My dad gave each of us some money, and we enjoyed various rides. I did not want to spend my money on something to eat. I wanted to spend it on rides and things to see.

Our visit to the Natatorium was a pleasant experience except for one incident. While I was watching a juggler performing in a large tent, a white man got angry with me. He pushed me to the ground. He started calling me a Jap as I sat in the sawdust, stunned. A number of hostile stares were directed at me from several people in the tent. The manager told me to leave, and as I was being escorted out, my dad, Luana, and Bernard walked up. My dad asked what was wrong. When he found out that the people thought I was a Jap, he explained, "My boy is not a Jap. He is an Indian." The manager looked at me and said he guessed that was better than being a Jap. Everyone calmed down after that. I was not offended by the incident, but I was surprised. I wondered why the man thought I was a Jap.

We spent another night at the hotel. When morning came, my dad cranked the Model T as I adjusted the gas and spark. Brownie jumped up on the right front fender, and we headed back to Manila Creek. We arrived about six hours later and prepared to leave for the Inchelium area.

After loading our belongings into the Model T, my dad looked into the house one more time. He wanted to make sure we had packed everything we wanted to take. We got the car started, and minutes later, we were descending into the Sanpoil area. It was the first of August, and the weather was very hot. When we reached the small town of Keller, we crossed the Sanpoil River and headed east. We were going to take the Silver Creek road to Inchelium. We were in no hurry to reach Inchelium and stopped at a number of familiar places that we had not seen for some time. Brownie inspected these areas and re-marked his territory. Clearly, he remembered these places and was happy to be back.

10 / Moving On

We finally arrived in the Inchelium area about five hours later. We drove another six miles to reach the Lincoln Lumber Company camp. The company manager had reserved a two-room cabin for us. It was next to a large pond, and when I learned that the pond was full of eastern brook trout, I was excited. I had never before caught an eastern brook. Upper Hall Creek was about a half mile away, and I was anxious to see if the fishing was good there.

Loggers and their families were moving into the camp daily. I counted about twenty-five cabins when we arrived, and space was being cleared for more. The cookhouse was nearly completed, but the water system still required additional work. Meanwhile, a small creek flowing about 200 feet away supplied everyone with drinking water. The loggers' wives paid me to pack water for them. This kept me busy for about two weeks until the well and water supply were ready for use. I made enough spending money in that time to buy clothes for school.

After my job of packing water ended, I got out my fishing tackle and explored Upper Hall Creek. The fishing in the pond was good, but it was best after sunset. The eastern brook fought well once they were hooked. They were larger and heavier than the trout in Hall Creek. There were many water snakes and blue racers near the pond, but no rattlesnakes, and I was relieved to know that.

The summer went by quickly at Upper Hall Creek, and we enjoyed the area. When I was not fishing, I explored the hills and mountains with my .22 Stevens. September came, and Luana, Bernard, and I entered school in Inchelium. The school had been moved from Old Inchelium and was about two miles south of our house on its one acre of land. The building had been dismantled and put back together in its new location. The gymnasium had also been moved and was located next to the school.

Before the People moved from Old Inchelium, disagreement arose between them. They split into two factions: those who moved to the Cobb's Creek area, where our house and property was, and those who moved to the Skunk Flat area, about two miles south. These people argued about where the new town of Inchelium should be located. No one could agree, so the Catholic church and the sub-agency were placed in the Cobb's Creek area, while the school, store, and post office were located in Skunk Flat. Both areas claimed to be the new Inchelium. For awhile, both sides had little to do with each other. It took a few years before people finally forgot those intense feelings and disagreements of the past.

A bus picked us up and brought us back from the school in Inchelium. Bernard was excited about entering the first grade. He made friends easily with his classmates. But after the first day of school, I was disappointed to find that the school had not changed much in the time since I had been there for my first three years. It was not uncommon for some students to ridicule the teachers and the principal. Sometimes the principal had to manhandle certain students to maintain order. This was disruptive for the rest of us, who were trying to learn. Despite my disappointment, I was pleased to be with old friends and relatives whom I had not seen in more than three years. We had all grown and changed in many ways during that time.

When I was not in school, I drifted back to my old ways of entertaining myself by seeking solitude. I spent most of my time by myself, devoting long hours to fishing, hunting, or going for long walks in the mountains. It was a good way to escape my problems, to clear my mind and think. Thoughts of my grandfather, White Grizzly Bear, always came to me when I was in the forests, hills, and mountains. I tried to move softly, without making any noise. I knew my grandfather had disciplined himself to do that when he walked the forests or hunted for large game.

Sometimes, when I was alone, I thought of Chemawa and the happenings I had enjoyed there. I missed the coffee breaks and the talks about tribes and their distinctive ways. I remembered discussing great leaders and warriors and the battles against the cavalry, when courage and fighting skills were displayed. The stories told by the Indians from Montana and South Dakota had always impressed me. I truly admired the Blackfeet, Lakota, Cheyenne, and Pawnee. No one seemed to think or talk about those Indians in Inchelium.

There did not seem to be any identifiable traditional Indian ways within our tribe. We seemed to carry on with a process of living that focused only on surviving from day to day. I wondered how different we present-day Lakes Indians were from the Sin-Aikst of the past.

Only the elders could speak our language. Only a few could identify areas in the hills where certain roots and plants grew that were used for eating or as medicines. I could not think of anyone who knew how to sing or dance in the traditional way or spoke of the spirits or their powers.

We lost so much of our way of life when Kettle Falls was flooded over with the completion of Grand Coulee Dam. We no longer lived together in bands. The last community that resembled a band was Old Inchelium. We now lived apart, in isolated areas of the hills and lower mountains. The cohesiveness that once existed within the bands had maintained patterns of living that were hundreds of years old. We were gradually losing our tribal identity. We were losing a way of life that had kept our forebears content and united for centuries.

One day at the end of September, my mother appeared at the school. She came at noon so we were free to visit awhile. We were surprised but very pleased to see her. She looked at us with a big smile on her face. She told us that we had all grown so much in the three years since we had last seen her at Chemawa in October 1940. She had changed only a little. She looked happy and healthy.

We found a quiet place away from the rest of our classmates and talked of many things. We learned that she was still living in Tacoma, Washington, and was working in Harry Wong's restaurant. Our mother told us she had married Harry after they left Grand Coulee Dam and moved to Tacoma. They had a nice restaurant, and business was good. She told us that most of the people who came to the restaurant were women. Servicemen also stopped in occasionally. She told us there were many soldiers in Tacoma because it was close to Fort Lewis.

My mother said she was still trying to get the court to allow her to take care of us. She said that in the meantime, she would ask the court to let the three of us visit her in Tacoma during the summer. My mother had never given up hope that one day we would live together again.

She told us she had to return to Tacoma in a few days because Harry needed her help in the restaurant. We were told to take care of one another and study hard in school. She was pleased that we were back home. She hugged and kissed the three of us, and then she left. We did not know it then, but we would not see her again for two years. Seeing our mother always gave us hope and the strength to go on. When she was with us, we forgot about the times we had spent without her. We always sensed that we would see her again and things would be fine.

Men in uniform were often seen in the Inchelium area. They always attracted attention. The servicemen's uniforms were all clean and pressed. Their hair was cut short and their shoes were highly polished. I remembered that my shoes had also been polished during my years at Chemawa. Almost all the young men were now in the service. Many had seen action, and some had been killed overseas. Young boys who were not quite old enough could hardly wait to enlist. They felt it was important to be in uniform.

Winter came, bringing heavy snowfall. The tree-covered mountains were beautiful, and the world seemed very peaceful. I enjoyed getting out and going for long walks in the snow. I learned to enjoy the beauty of quiet. The area around us took on a new dimension with the presence of snow.

When Christmas came, I enjoyed listening to the Christmas carols that played repeatedly on the radio. As always, presents were delivered from our mother, and we sent presents to her for the first time in many years. We were happy to be able to do this. In January, it got very cold. We did not venture out much during the cold spell, so we either studied or listened to the radio. Sometimes I heard classical music and listened with interest. I was beginning to like this kind of music very much. The cold did not seem to bother my dad. He was not a man to spend time indoors. He always found work out of doors, regardless of the temperature.

Finally, the weather changed, and about the first of March, it was warm enough to resume my walks in the hills and lower mountains. One day, while I was hiking up in the hills, I saw about thirty-five wild horses. I was unable to get close to them, but they were beautiful to watch from a distance as they ran up and down through a small valley. The next day, I returned, but they would not let me get close, even with grass in my hand. After school, on the third day, I came to within about thirty feet of them. Then, on the fourth day, one of the horses approached and took the grass from my hand, then galloped away. On the fifth day, late in the afternoon, three of them came up to me and allowed me to feed them and pet their necks. I maintained a calm and quiet manner because I did not want to frighten them.

When I visited with them later in the spring, the whole herd came to me and allowed me to walk among them. I was impressed not only with their beauty but with the freedom and joy of life they expressed while being in the hills.

After fishing for most of the morning one day, I decided to go home early and work on my bicycle. The brakes needed adjusting, and I thought I could make the necessary repairs with my dad's tools. I had caught a dozen trout, enough for our dinner that night. To save time, I decided to cut across a large alfalfa field to reach the road that led to the camp.

An irrigation ditch ran alongside me. It was totally covered in places by the heavy growth of alfalfa. As I walked, I cast my line into an open spot in the ditch. A large fish bit the hook and yanked me to one side. I was taken off guard and surprised at the weight of the fish, but I managed to land it. It was a large rainbow, more than twenty inches in length. This was the largest fish I had ever seen next to the salmon at Kettle Falls. I put a new grasshopper on my hook and cast it into the water again. There was an immediate tug on the line, and with some effort, I pulled another large rainbow out of the ditch. The second rainbow was at least three inches longer than the first. A wave of excitement came over me as I baited my hook with another grasshopper. A third large rainbow took the bait, and I pulled it in. It was about two inches longer than the first rainbow.

I was about to cast my line again when I saw a man yelling and running toward me. When he reached me, he told me I was trespassing on his property. He said I could keep the fish but I should leave at once and never come back. Years later, I learned that the man was Charlie Charette, the father of Francis and Tommy, who were my friends at Chemawa.

I reached the road that led to the camp. I had walked about a quarter of a mile when a station wagon with four white men in it drove by. The car came to an abrupt stop, and the driver put the car in reverse and backed toward me. The men jumped out of their car and wanted to look at the fish I had caught. They were excited about the size of the rainbow. They asked me where I had caught them, and one wanted to look at my old pole. My pole had been in my possession for almost five years. I had found an old metal telescopic pole, rubbed off most of the rust, and taped it together with some of my dad's black tape. About seven feet of fishing line was tied to the end, and a spinner with two round sinkers was secured eight inches above the hook. The white man dismissed my pole with a shrug and gave it back to me.

The men asked if they could look at the bait. I carried my bait in an old tobacco can in my back pocket. I removed the can from my pocket and handed it to one of the men. I told them that I usually used red-winged grasshoppers but I had run out. When they asked again where I had caught the large rainbow, I told my first lie. I said I caught the rainbow at Upper Hall Creek, about two miles from where we were standing. The men thanked me and jumped hastily into their station wagon. They started the motor and took off very fast in the direction of Upper Hall Creek.

One day during May, I saw a squirrel carrying what looked like a mouse in her mouth. I was curious, so I chased it. When the squirrel reached the base of a pine tree, it dropped what it was carrying and ran up the tree. The squirrel chattered angrily at me as I looked at the little animal. I realized that it was a baby squirrel. Its eyes were still closed and it could barely move. I picked the baby up and studied it while the mother continued to chatter angrily at me. If I had known better, I would have left the baby alone with its mother, but I didn't. I returned home with the little one.

I showed the baby to my dad. He told me to open a can of milk and mix it with some warm water and a small amount of sugar. Then he took a small dropper from an eye drops bottle and filled it with the milk-and-water mixture. He picked up the baby squirrel in his left hand and put the end of the dropper into the baby's mouth. The young one immediately grasped the dropper tube with its front feet and began to gulp the mixture down. I was surprised and pleased that the baby squirrel would feed so readily.

From that time, I continued to feed the young squirrel five times a day for approximately a week. The squirrel's eyes opened after about five days, and it showed noticeable growth. Three weeks later, I started to feed the squirrel bread and crackers. When the squirrel was six weeks old, I also fed it pine nuts.

The squirrel followed me constantly and soon learned to crawl up and sit on my shoulders while I rode my bicycle. Later, when I went swimming in the Columbia with friends, the squirrel played in the trees that bordered the river. It came to me when it was time to go home.

People who visited us were always surprised at how friendly and tame the squirrel was. They found it hard to believe that the squirrel always returned to me after playing in the trees. I learned one day that the squirrel loved peanut-butter sandwiches. While I was eating one, he jumped onto my lap, tore off a piece of my sandwich, and ate it. We shared many peanut-butter sandwiches from that day on.

I did not know that my dad had written Judge Brown inquiring about job possibilities in the Okanogan area. One day in early July, my dad received a letter from Judge Brown. He advised my dad that the apple growers were expecting a heavy crop in the fall and were going to need help with the harvest.

Jim Wade Orchards was planning to hire many Mexicans and needed someone to interpret for them since no one there could speak Spanish. Judge Brown knew that my dad was fluent in Spanish and would be interested in the job. He contacted Jim Wade Orchards, and they offered my dad a job as interpreter for the fall season.

My dad told us he had gotten the job in the Okanogan area and we should be prepared to leave in about a week. He also said that we would be going to school at Okanogan in the fall. Luana and I were surprised by the news. I was concerned about getting along at an all-white school.

We knew a few students at Inchelium who were white, but we had grown up with them. We accepted them almost as members of the tribe. The more I thought about it, the more I anticipated trouble. I was glad that I had learned the principles of boxing at Chemawa and decided to practice every day so I could get better. Shadowboxing and the calisthenics I had learned at Chemawa became part of my daily routine. I wanted to be prepared for any trouble that might come my way.

Our people had always been aware of the boundaries of the reservation, and we knew only a little about the towns that bordered it. We knew that the students who went to the schools outside the reservation were white. We were not concerned, because we were content to live in our own world with our own people. Whites joined our communities little by little. We accepted them and treated them with fairness and respect. We expected them to treat us in the same manner. Our people had lost much to the whites over the years. We had adjusted to a way of life and a standard of living that we knew were much different from those of the whites.

One day, we were driving in the mountains near Gold Mountain and saw a deer standing under some trees. The deer was about 500 feet from the road. My dad stopped the Model T and told me we could use the meat. He asked me if I thought I could hit it with my .22 from that distance. I had never shot a deer before, and I was unsure if my .22 would carry that far.

My first shot missed, and the deer turned to run up the mountain. I quickly inserted another shell and fired again. The second shot found its mark, and I realized I had just gotten my first deer. My dad butchered the deer on the spot. He wrapped the pieces of meat in paper and placed them in burlap sacks. We had more meat than we could eat, so we shared some with our neighbors at the camp.

The next day, a friend of my dad told him there was a car for sale and the price was low because the owner needed the money. Our Model T was getting very old, so my dad was interested. He decided to take a look at the car and told us he would be gone for a while. My dad's friend said they could go in his car.

A day later, my dad returned driving a 1929 Model A Ford. Compared to the Model T, it looked like a new car. The three of us got into the car, impressed that it had four doors. The Model A had comfortable seats that were covered with a fabric that was soft to the touch. There were a few holes and worn areas here and there, since the car was fifteen years old, but we paid no attention to that. Our dad took us for a ride, and we noticed that the car ran smoothly and the motor had an even sound. I was impressed when I found that I could roll the windows up and down. We were not able to do this in the Model T. It was exciting for all three of us to know we would each have a place to sit when riding in the car.

We looked the car over and discovered some rust spots here and there. My dad spit out his snoose and said he was going to buy some paint for the Model A. Meanwhile, he took sandpaper from his toolbox and showed me how to sand out the rust spots. I spent the rest of the day sanding the car, and the next day my dad bought some kelly green paint. He also bought two paintbrushes.

It took us about seven hours, but the car looked like it was new when we were finished. It was the brightest-colored car in the Inchelium area. We were pleased with the results and ready to go to Okanogan. This was the first time in my life that I felt I was coming up in the world because I owned something.

We started packing while the paint on the Model A was drying. My dad had to purchase an old trailer to hold all of our belongings. We slept that night in the cabin by the pond, and it was the last night that we would sleep as a family on the reservation.

Before we left for Okanogan, my dad drove the Model T to our house at Cobb's Creek. A friend followed in his car, so he could give my dad and me a ride back to our cabin. I rode with my dad in the Model T.

When we reached our house, I opened the gate so my dad could park the Model T next to the shed.

He jacked up the Model T and set the front and rear axles on blocks. Then he removed the four wheels and placed them in the shed. He covered the Model T with a canvas tarp. While he was doing this, I walked down to the creek. I got a shovel and dug up angleworms. I threw them into the creek and watched the trout eat. The trout had grown over the years and enjoyed the area I had cleared in the creek. I had a feeling that this would be the last time I would see them. I watched as they swam easily in the water. I returned to the shed as my dad finished tying the tarp to the Model T.

This was the last time I would see the Model T. This car was more than a vehicle for travel. It had been an important part of our family since I was born. Thoughts of our past, with the Model T, came back to me. We had traveled together over almost every road on the reservation. Many times, our journeys lasted beyond the daylight hours. We did not measure time by the clock. Sometimes, on the spur of the moment, my dad loaded us into the Model T and took us somewhere. Luana, Bernard, and I always looked forward to forthcoming adventures.

When we traveled at night, we had new experiences. There were always deer on the roads. Sometimes, we saw bear, grouse, and rabbits, and more than once, a rattlesnake crawled across the road as the Model T labored forward. Sometimes the grades were too steep for the Model T, but my dad learned that the car could climb steep hills in reverse, so he would turn the car around and back up the hill. My dad always packed food in the bed of the Model T. Bread, soda crackers, peanut butter, honey, and canned fish such as tuna, salmon, and sardines were always part of our food supplies. Sometimes, we were lucky and found butterhorns and donuts in the back, too. We saved them for dessert.

If we were stranded somewhere by the late hour or car trouble, we were not concerned. We unloaded our food supplies and, if it was dark, lit the gas lamp to enjoy dinner under the trees and stars. Afterward, we prepared our bedding by placing burlap sacks on the wild grass. We covered these with the assortment of blankets that was always packed away for such emergencies in the bed of the Model T. My thoughts dwelled on those good times as we said good-bye to our old friend.

Early in the morning, we prepared to leave for Okanogan. Brownie did not want to ride on the front fender of the Model A, so we had to make room for him inside the car. With the squirrel and another dog, Snooks, who was part cocker spaniel, our family had grown to seven, and it was crowded in the car.

We drove past Twin Lakes and Gold Mountain to reach the Sanpoil, then crossed Bridge Creek and turned north to pass Westport. When we reached the town of Republic, we were off the reservation. We knew that from now on, we would be working and living in the midst of white people. We turned west at Republic and headed for Wauconda. Beyond Wauconda, we came to Pickles's gravesite, and I paid my respects to my first friend whom we had buried in November 1937, seven years before. Finally we reached Tonasket. There were apple orchards everywhere and many white people working in the orchards. Tonasket was not a large town, but it was big compared to Inchelium. There were all types of stores and places to eat and drink beer, but what attracted me most was a movie theater.

My dad told us we were going to stay in Tonasket for a few weeks and thin apples in the orchards because we were low on money. We found an orchard that needed workers on the other side of the Okanogan River, about four miles south. The owner of the orchard showed us a cabin where we could stay, and the next day, we were working. Luana and I helped our dad, and he showed us how to thin the apples. Luana and I were not paid for our work. We could not lift or move the ladders easily because they were too heavy. It was a good experience, however, because we would be thinning apples during the summer for the next five years.

While the three of us worked, Bernard stayed near the cabin with Brownie, Snooks, and the squirrel. They entertained themselves until my dad, Luana, and I returned to prepare supper. The weather was especially hot in the orchards because breezes could not flow easily through the apple trees. As the days went by, we adjusted to conditions in the orchard. We found asparagus growing wild near the orchards and gathered it to eat with our supper after work.

One night while we ate supper, an Indian woman appeared. She offered us half of a pie she had baked. We thanked her and ate it for dessert. We had not eaten a pie for years and relished the tasty crust and the peaches inside. My dad said she came from Nespelem and he knew her family. He said they were good people.

Late one afternoon, after work, I took my .22 and went looking for a place to practice shooting. I walked into the hills for about a mile. A two-point whitetail buck appeared, loping down a valley. I decided we needed meat, so I stalked the buck for about a half hour, then fired off a clean shot. I ran back to the cabin to get my dad so he could help dress the deer and carry it back to the cabin.

The deer was small, but there was more meat than we could handle. We shared the rest of the deer with other Indians who were also working at the orchard. An Indian man walked over to me and said that I had better be careful about hunting deer off the reservation. He told me that white people could hunt only during the deer-hunting season and he thought the required license cost money. He said I had broken the law but he would not tell on me. He rolled a cigarette and lit it. He laughed and walked back to his cabin.

When some of the Indians at the orchard learned that our family was moving to Okanogan, they asked if it was wise. They told my dad to expect resentment from the white people. They went on to say that friends of theirs had experienced prejudice in both Omak and Okanogan and that Indians were not welcome in the white communities.

My dad spit out his snoose and went into the cabin to get his pipe. When he was working, he chewed snoose, but he always sought out his pipe when he had important things to think about or say. He put tobacco into the bowl and tamped it. When it was firmly packed, he lit it with a match. He puffed awhile, and as the smoke curled upward, he said, "What they say is true. Life is going to be different. The white man does things in different ways. We are going to have to obey rules that do not exist on the reservation." He sat down on an apple box in the shade nearby. "We will not be around our friends or people anymore. We will be living and working where the white man is. Many of them will not like us because we are Indian. We will have to live with that."

I told my dad, "I wish we could stay in Inchelium. I don't think we will like living away from there." I thought of the fall of 1937, when we had camped at the orchard near Omak. I remembered how the white men harassed our family as our dad and mother picked apples near our tent. I wondered if we would have to experience that treatment again. "We know the people at home," I continued. "We know the country, and I think we can survive if we all work together. I know we will be happier with our people and friends."

My dad answered, "I know, but there is no work there. I have to work to support us. I have to make money and earn a living for all of us." I nodded as Luana and Bernard listened quietly. Brownie, Snooks, and the squirrel seemed to be listening, too. Luana always listened thoughtfully when our dad and I discussed plans for the family. Once we decided on a plan of action, Luana and Bernard did their best to help make it work.

My dad's decisions were usually correct. When they did not turn out well for the family, we did not belabor the point. We always did our best to make the best of every situation. Our family always worked together to make each day a good one.

We did not have to work on Sundays, so my dad took the three of us to the theater in Tonasket to see a matinee. We tied Brownie and Snooks outside the cabin and left the squirrel inside. There were no theaters on the reservation, so watching a movie was a special treat for us, and we always enjoyed it, no matter what the subject.

After apple thinning was over in July, we loaded the Model A and the trailer and prepared to leave for Okanogan. We said good-bye to the Indians we had met and wished them well. They wished us well in return. We also said farewell to a way of life that we would never experience again. As we drove away from the orchard, the Indians waved to us. I had a strange, wistful feeling. Normally, I looked forward to visiting new places and having new adventures. But this time, I did not feel that anticipation or interest.

We reached the paved highway and turned south, following the Okanogan River. I knew that something special had ended. I sensed that relatives, friends, and places dear to me would not be close again. I felt we were on the verge of losing something important, a culture and a way of life that had always been a mainstay of the People.

Luana, Bernard, and I had gotten older, but we felt older than we actually were. It seemed we had lived a long time and experienced many things. We were sad about leaving our people and our homeland. I felt apprehensive and alone as I thought about trying to survive in the white man's world. The good times had passed, and another way of life faced us. Our childhood was over.

11 / Okanogan

After our family left Tonasket, we traveled to Okanogan. I was thirteen, Luana eleven, and Bernard six years old. We crossed a masonry bridge over the Okanogan River to reach the town of Okanogan. The bridge connected the Colville Indian Reservation to Okanogan. I thought of the differences that existed at each end of the bridge. The bridge separated two cultures that had conflicting values. It separated a people who had grown and gained materially from a people who were repressed and struggling to survive. Luana, Bernard, and I were hesitant about crossing the bridge. I believe we sensed we were going to lose something important when we did. Learning and surviving in the white man's world would come at a high cost.

We drove through the main street. Everyone I saw was white. There were no Indians. I noticed the stores, gas stations, restaurants, taverns, a barbershop, and a bank. There were at least two hotels and a large movie theater. The people in town seemed to stare at us as we drove down the main street. I felt out of place and as if I did not belong to the area.

I hoped our stay in Okanogan would be short. I prayed that conditions would change on the reservation so we could return home to Inchelium. I knew that our Way had been badly hurt, and there were doubts that it would ever recover. But I questioned whether I would be able to adjust to the white man's world. I wondered if efforts to adjust would be worth it. I thought of relatives and friends back in Inchelium and how we lived our lives. I began to miss home.

We drove to the Jim Wade Orchards and moved into two small concrete-block cabins. The four of us slept in one cabin and used the other one to prepare meals, eat, and do our schoolwork. The cabins had electric lights but no running water or heat. We purchased and installed a wood-burning heater with a flat top that we could cook on and burned wood cut from dead apple trees. We purchased a small electric heater for our sleeping cabin. During the winter, Brownie and Snooks slept in the cabin where we prepared meals, and the squirrel slept on the overhead rafters with us.

That fall, my dad worked as the interpreter for the Mexican laborers and the foremen. I was surprised at how well he spoke Spanish. I had never heard him speak it before. There were more than 250 Mexicans who lived in a large warehouse close to our cabins. I enjoyed trying to communicate with them. After work, they brought out their guitars and played and sang Mexican music. My dad joined them on his guitar, and many of the workers came to listen and enjoy the music. We were surrounded by 500 acres of apple orchards, and this became our new home.

In the fall of 1944, we entered the Okanogan school. Luana and I were the only nonwhites there. I felt isolated. Outwardly, no one seemed to resent our presence; nevertheless, we were ignored. Bernard was enrolled in the grade school at Malott, a small community seven miles south of Okanogan, which he traveled to and from in a small school bus. The schoolwork at Okanogan was hard for me, and it was difficult to keep up with the white students. The three of us buried ourselves in our studies. We avoided special school activities that required payment, because we could not afford them. When we had some spending money, movies at the Avalon Theatre became our escape and favored pastime.

Gradually, I grew to understand the studies at school. I learned to keep up with my white classmates, although we were never able to match their way of life. We were only partially accepted and did not participate in the social activities that were so popular with all the others in Okanogan.

During the summer, Luana and I worked in the orchards. We thinned apples six days a week. The work was hard, and the weather was hot. Bernard filled water bags with cold water and brought them to us daily. The water was a welcome relief. In the fall, we picked apples with our dad. The work seemed to last forever on cold days. Bernard wanted to help us, but only the high school students had time off for the harvest, and he had to go to school. The combined income of my dad, Luana, and me helped get us through the year.

The orchards provided work for only six months out of the year, and there was no other work during the cold months. I was not able to fish, and hunting was not good across the river, on the reservation. I could not add to our food supplies as I had on the reservation in Inchelium. My dad knew that our income from the working season would not carry us through the winter months. We would have to obtain food in other ways.

One day, my dad talked to the owner of the grocery store in Okanogan where we bought our food. He found out that vegetables and fruit that were not salable were placed out in the alley every other night. My dad, realizing that this was our only food source, collected vegetables such as potatoes, carrots, cabbage, and lettuce if they were not totally spoiled. He cut away the spoiled parts and saved what was edible. He salvaged fruit like oranges, bananas, and grapes in the same manner. We survived on this food until he was able to find work in the orchards in late spring of the following year.

This was a difficult and embarrassing way for us to live. We had always been able to get food by hunting or fishing or by working for it. Taking discarded food was foreign to us. We did not earn it by working for it. It seemed no different from begging, but we had no choice. When we left Inchelium, we expected to improve our situation, but we found that living in the Okanogan area was not much better than living on the reservation in Inchelium. There was more work in Okanogan, and the pay was better, but there were more expenses.

Before coming to Okanogan, I never thought about poverty. I did not know the meaning of the word or what it meant to be poor. In Okanogan, I began to understand its meaning through the eyes of white people. I was aware that our family did not have as much money. We did not own an expensive car or a large home. We could not afford costly things. Our possessions were few.

When we lived in Inchelium, our family did not measure wealth in terms of money. We believed that richness came from being able to experience and appreciate things created by the Great Spirit. The ability to know and cherish relatives and good friends was also important. We believed it was enough to be healthy and enjoy each day from first light to late night. White people, we found, viewed the appreciation of wealth in another way.

For people who could afford it, there were more things to do in Okanogan. There were also more things to buy. Luana and I worked as long as we could in the orchards so we could buy some of the things we wanted from stores in Okanogan and Omak. Yet we continued to salvage vegetables and fruit during the cold months of every year. Finally, three years later, my dad was able to get full-time work as a section hand on the Great Northern Railway in Okanogan. Life was better for us from that time on.

Schoolwork was never easy for me, and I spent long hours trying to keep up with the other students. At a class in music appreciation, I learned about the history of classical music. I was introduced to the great composers and learned about the music that had impressed me very much when I lived on the reservation. It was a revelation to me, and it pleases me still to have an understanding of these great composers and their works. As an artist years later, I always listened to classical music while I worked. The music transformed my energy and complemented my creativity, enabling me to work creatively for long periods of time.

I also developed some "Yankee ingenuity" as I worked in the orchards and apple-packing sheds, where there were a variety of machines to operate and maintain. Over the years, I learned how to run and repair them.

The three of us approached maturity at the end of our years in Okanogan. We knew that our way of life as Indians had been altered by the white culture, and we were somewhat confused by the lives we were living. We did not know it then, but everything we had learned in the last decade, our studies in school and our experiences in the orchards of Okanogan, would help us very much in our later lives.

12 / Farewell

Powerful Kettle Falls blurred and began to fade away. I tried to maintain my focus on the wondrous scene that had been before me. The roar of the falls and the echoes of people shouting and talking also passed. It was as if the spirits had gone. In their place was a large lake and then nothing but quiet. An immense body of water covered the falls. It did not move, and it was lifeless. My drifting thoughts returned to the present. I felt I was awakening from a long dream into feelings of despair and loneliness. I realized that I had been standing there and thinking for a long time.

The sun was setting and the shadows of the tall pine trees grew very long. The cawing of crows could be heard in the distance. The wind blowing through the branches above added life to the trees. The shadows shimmered as they reached for the lake. It seemed as if they were struggling to restore life as it once had been.

It was hard for me to accept that such a great way of life had ended. I could not understand why the beautiful blending of earth, water, and beings could no longer exist. It was difficult to accept the thinking of those who allowed this to happen. I was certain that the people who had planned this destruction had little sense of history, beauty, or life.

As I stood there, I felt very old. I realized I was weary. Poco was gazing up at me. He looked concerned, and I reached down to stroke his head and ears. He bit my hand playfully as he always did, and I told him it was time to go.

As we turned to walk back to the car, a young white man approached us. "What were you looking at out there?" he asked with interest. "Kettle Falls," I answered, "or where Kettle Falls used to be."

"I've heard of the falls," he said, "but I never knew exactly where it was."

I pointed to the area where three levels of Kettle Falls had existed. I described the location of Hayes Island and a smaller island that lay northeast of it. "My people used to camp there to dry and smoke the salmon they caught. In earlier days, special canoes from upriver were everywhere, and that's how people got across the river. The tribes assembled in June of each year to catch their main food supply," I went on. "As a boy, I would stand in wonder as the chinooks, some more than a hundred pounds in weight, leaped the churning falls."

I reached into the pocket of my jacket for a cigarette. "I still recall the roar of the falls and the voices of the people shouting instructions to each other. I'll never forget the beauty of the hundreds of tepees of the different tribes. They lined the shores of the river close to the falls. There were horses and people everywhere."

"That must have been something to see," the young man said thoughtfully.

"Yes," I answered, reaching for Poco. "It was beautiful. Kettle Falls was once the center of our people's culture. It was special to behold."

Epilogue

Luana, Bernard, and I graduated from Okanogan High School and moved west of the mountains to live in Tacoma with our mother. We had no idea of the roles we would play in the future.

After I left Okanogan, I was able to work my way through college. During those years, I met Joyce Meachem, and we became friends. She was a Yakama and Warm Springs Indian on her father's side. The late George Meachem was chief of the Warm Springs Indians in Oregon. Margaret Sampson Ross, a Swinomish from the Bow Hill area near Bellingham, is Joyce's mother. In 1955, Joyce and I were married.

While I was in the Seattle-Tacoma area, I tried to find my direction in life. In December 1954, I joined the U.S. Army. After completing basic training at Fort Ord, California, I was sent to Worms, Germany, near the Rhine River. I became part of the 12th A.I.B., Second Armored Division, U.S. Army. I spent eleven months on active duty, then decided to take leave time and travel in Europe.

My tour of Europe took me to Florence, Venice, Rome, and Pompeii in Italy. Later, I traveled in France, to Paris and Rheims, and to London. I also visited Amsterdam, Copenhagen, Malmo in Sweden, and most of West Germany. During these trips, I studied architectural wonders closely and was able to appreciate them. The interiors of the Roman residences in Pompeii, dating from the great days of the Roman empire, impressed me very much. I was also able to view great works of art by European masters. I knew then that I would pursue the related fields of architecture, design, and art.

I returned to Tacoma, and Joyce and I moved to Seattle. I entered the University of Washington, where I received instruction in painting and sculpture from several fine teachers. I also benefited from the guidance and inspiration offered by Professor Hope Foote when I chose interior design as my major. In 1957, Joyce and I had a son, Darren, and what spare time we had was devoted to him.

Although I admired Western contemporary art, I sensed I should direct my efforts to a type of art that was related to my heritage. I was impressed with Pacific North Coast art and how it drew inspiration from the beings of the forest and water. This matched the closeness and respect I felt for them, which I had inherited from my grandfather, White Grizzly Bear. Pacific North Coast art and philosophy inspired me and helped me develop a style of art that I could call my own.

I work mostly with wood. White pine, alder, and cedar seem to be best for me. The beings of the forest and water are the subjects of all my work. I believe there is life in a piece of wood, regardless of its size. If I study the wood long enough, I can sense the being inside. I work until it is released and takes its form. The Pacific North Coast carvers felt the same way when they created their great totems and war canoes. These carvers of the past provided direction for my work.

In 1960, I met Maxine Cushing Gray. She was the art editor of *Argus* magazine in Seattle and had an extensive knowledge of fine art. She was also interested in the art of the American Indian. We met several times and discussed Indian art at length. Maxine was interested in the directions my art was taking.

Over the years, she observed and printed several articles about my work, which led to more articles in the *Seattle Post-Intelligencer, Seattle Times,* and *Puget Soundings* magazine. Soon after, I received important coverage on television.

While I was employed at the Seafirst Corporation as a designer, several commissions came from companies with ties to Seafirst. This kept me very active artistically. In 1964, Joyce gave birth to our daughter, Lara Lin.

For twenty-five years, I spent my days working on projects for Seafirst in the United States, Europe, and Asia, I worked on my own art commissions in the evenings and on weekends. Media coverage from newspapers and television stimulated interest in my work among other corporations and the public. My work sold more easily, and I was also able to form close ties with art organizations such as the Seattle Arts Commission and the Washington State Arts Commission.

For my last seven years with Seafirst, I served as the art director in charge of creating and curating the Seafirst Corporate Art Collection. I traveled to Chicago, Los Angeles, New York, and San Francisco to purchase important paintings and sculpture for the collection. The collection grew to more than 2,000 works, and the media provided favorable coverage over the years.

Museums such as the Museum of Modern Art in San Francisco, the Corcoran in Washington, D.C., and the Museum of Modern Art in Montgomery, Alabama, requested loans from the Seafirst collection for exhibition in their cities. Gallaudet College in Washington, D.C., requested a loan of several works to be displayed on their campus.

Several interested groups in the Northwest requested time to view the collection. Early in 1981, a number of patrons came from Los Angeles to see the works, as did a large group from New York at the end of 1981. David Rockefeller, chairman of the board of Chase Manhattan Bank in New York, requested a personal tour that same year when he visited

Seattle. Earlier, Mr. Rockefeller had shared with me information on corporate art collecting that helped me create the Seafirst Corporate Art Collection.

In my free time, I created more than 600 works of sculpture for residences and for other corporations connected with Seafirst. Some of my strongest works are now in England, Switzerland, Iceland, and Japan. When the right jobs appeared, I provided interior design services for homes and businesses on a freelance basis.

Over the years, I received first-place awards from the Scottsdale National Art Exhibition in Arizona, the Philbrook Art Center in Tulsa, and the Center for Indian Art in Washington, D.C. In 1970, the University of Washington approached me and asked if I would teach an art course. Since my job schedules were heavy, we agreed that I would teach an evening course called Contemporary Indian Art.

In 1970, one of my sculptures was selected to represent the state of Washington at the World's Fair in Osaka, Japan. I received the 1972 Governor's Art Award for sculpture in Washington State. From 1976 through 1980, I served as commissioner of the Seattle Arts Commission, with responsibilities of selecting art for sites and buildings owned and managed by the City of Seattle. In 1982, Governor Daniel Evans appointed me to the Governor's Art Task Force to help plan the arts appropriation budget for the state of Washington. In 1983, I received the Peace and Friendship Award for my contributions to American Indian Art in Washington State.

When our children were grown, Joyce decided to study for her master's in social work at the University of Washington. After graduation, she was elected president of the Indian Women's Service League. In that post, she was effective in helping Bernard unite the various Indian organizations and tribes in Seattle. It was important to present a united front in dealing with the City of Seattle, Washington State, and the federal government.

Joyce was appointed the first Indian director of the Yakama Indian

Health Center in Toppenish in 1990. She later became assistant director of the Indian Health Services Regional offices in Portland, Oregon, in 1993. In 1994, she received the highest award from the University of Washington Master's Graduate Program in Social Work at a special ceremony in Seattle. This was a tribute to her work and her contributions to her field since she had received her master's degree in 1973.

In 1984, I decided to take early retirement and resigned from Seafirst. I wanted to spend time traveling and visiting Indian tribes throughout the United States and Canada. After my granddaughters Gaby and Recy were born in 1992 and 1994, I spent time with them. I felt it was important to establish strong bonds with them from an early age. In 1999, Helen Adonay, Darren's wife, gave birth to my first grandson, Sebb. I now have three grandchildren to care for and concentrate on.

Luana graduated from high school in 1951 and moved to Tacoma to live with our mother. She worked for a department store, and at night, she was a part-time waitress at Harry Wong's restaurant. Luana provided companionship and helped my mother with various projects. She should have gone on to a university, but it did not turn out that way. However, she chose her jobs well over the years.

In 1965, Luana gave birth to her daughter Kecia in Seattle. After spending twenty years in the private sector in San Francisco, Hawaii, and Seattle, she was appointed the executive director of the Seattle Indian Health Board in 1972. During her tenure, the organization grew from a staff of five people to almost two hundred. She was in charge for more than ten years, and administered the growth and success of the organization during that time.

Today, the Seattle Indian Health Board is considered the largest and most successful organization of its kind in the country. It serves as a role model for tribes and urban Indian centers throughout the continental United States.

In 1982, Everett Rhodes, the director of Indian Health Services headquartered in Rockville, Maryland, called Luana. She was offered an important position in the organization. Luana accepted, and she and Kecia moved to Rockville. Within a few years, she was appointed director of headquarters operations. The organization of 14,000 people administers overall healthcare to all Indians in the United States, except for Hawaii. Her position of assistant director was second only to that of the director of Indian Health Services. Shortly before her untimely death in November 2001, Luana received a Presidential Rank Award for $25,000 for Meritorious Executive of the Department of Health and Human Services.

Bernard graduated from Okanogan High School in 1955 and attended the University of Washington for one year. But he decided he needed to earn money, so he left the university. He enlisted in the 101st Airborne and trained to be a paratrooper. After he completed basic training, he became a Green Beret. He served for two years and returned to the Seattle-Tacoma area, where he fished for salmon in the Puyallup River with Bob Satiacum.

Bob, a Puyallup Indian, and others were fighting at the time for their rights on the Puyallup River. Billy Frank Jr., Janet McCloud, and the Al and Maiselle Bridges family were also fighting against Washington State and the sports fishermen. The fishing rights of the Nisqually Tribe were being threatened by the state.

Bernard learned much about the conflicts between these Western Washington tribes, the sportsmen, and the politicians at the state capital in Olympia. He felt it was important to help the Puyallup, Nisqually, and others who were facing oppression from the sportsmen and the state. Tribes that were fighting for fishing rights were continually harassed on the rivers by state authorities. There were often violent confrontations between the authorities and the Indians, most notably on the Nisqually River. Many times, state authorities confiscated fishing nets and other equipment used by the Indian fishermen.

Finally, in 1974, after a three-year trial, U.S. District Court Judge

George Boldt came down with a ruling that the tribes were entitled to half the harvestable salmon running through their traditional waters. Furthermore, the tribes became co-managers of the state's fisheries. This was a major victory for the Western Washington tribes that depended on salmon for their survival.

Bernard dedicated his life to improving the quality of life for all Indians in the Seattle-Tacoma area. This decision changed his life dramatically and took him in unexpected directions. Shortly afterward, he changed his surname to Whitebear to honor the memory of Pic Ah Kelowna (White Grizzly Bear), our grandfather. In 1970, Bernard became a founder of the Seattle Indian Health Board, which provided badly needed health services for the thousands of Indian people living in the Seattle area. Bernard was appointed its first executive director.

In 1970, Bernard learned that the City of Seattle was in line to acquire a large portion of land due to a reduction of the Fort Lawton army post. Bernard and other Indians in Seattle felt the Indians should also receive land, and they met with city officials to state their case. The city government refused to take the Indians seriously.

Bernard and others led raids on Fort Lawton when they realized their case was not going to be heard. Hundreds of Indians from various tribes supported Bernard. He also froze the status of the land at the federal level. Seattle officials finally agreed to share twenty acres of Fort Lawton with the Indians, who had organized as the United Indians of All Tribes Foundation (UIATF).

Bernard resigned his post as executive director of the Seattle Indian Health Board. Shortly afterward, he was elected chief executive officer of the UIATF. While Bernard was its CEO, the land was set aside for use by the UIATF for ninety-nine years.

In 1974, designs submitted by Arai, Jackson and Reyes, Architects and Designers, for the Daybreak Star Center were finally approved. I had earlier joined the architects Arai and Jackson to form a team that would plan and design the center. My job was to set forth the philosophy, nomenclature, and organizational needs of the UIATF. Gerald Arai and Clifford Jackson, the architects, designed the beautiful Daybreak Star Center and the surrounding landscape.

That same year, Wes Uhlman, the mayor of Seattle, appointed Bernard commissioner of the Seattle Arts Commission. Bernard's proposal for artwork to adorn the interior of the Daybreak Star Center received a grant of $80,000. The artwork was created by the foremost Indian artists in the United States.

Bernard later approached Governor Daniel Evans in Olympia, and after days of negotiation, the governor agreed to fund construction of the Daybreak Star Center with a grant of $1,000,000. This act inspired tribes in Washington State as well as corporations to supply materials such as logs, timber, and roofing to help complete the building.

The center opened in 1977. More than 3,000 people celebrated the event. The beautiful building, an important statement of Indian art and architecture, commands a spectacular view of Puget Sound. It serves as the headquarters of the UIATF.

Over the years, Bernard allied himself with important leaders of many tribes. He received backing and advice from respected and resourceful Indian spokesmen and leaders such as Joe Delacruz (Quinault), Mike Smith (Lakota), Vine Deloria (Lakota), Willard Bill (Muckleshoot), Roger Jim and Joe Jay Pinkham (Yakama), Billy Frank Jr. (Nisqually), Janet McCloud (Tulalip), and Vic Johns (Tlingit). These people were at Bernard's side, working with him and providing valuable tribal and urban Indian support. During their time together, they became the closest of friends, sharing important tribal know-how and wisdom.

Bernard also allied himself with Bob Santos, director of the Asian Coalition; Roberto Maestas, director of El Centro de La Raza; and Larry Gossett, founder of the Central Area Motivation Project and presently a King County Council member. Throughout the last thirty years, they assisted one another in pursuing and receiving funding from the Seattle city government. The efforts of the "Gang of Four" enhanced the quality of life for all minority citizens in Seattle.

Under Bernard's leadership, the UIATF came to administer and oversee the Ina Maka family program, education and employment services, planning and operations, child development center, ECEAP preschool, the La-ba-te-yah youth home, the I'Wa'Sil youth program, the elders' service program, and the Sacred Circle Art Gallery. At the end of every July, a large powwow is held near the Daybreak Star Center on the Great Circle. Many tribes from all over the United States and Canada participate.

As the executive director, Bernard managed to acquire important parcels of land for the UIATF. A quarter of a block in downtown Seattle at Second Avenue and Cherry is now owned by Indians. One acre of land, including the building that houses the La-ba-te-yah youth home, in the Crown Hill district is owned by the UIATF. The Yale Building and land near Lake Union houses the organization's administrative offices. This complex has been owned and used for more than ten years by the UIATF.

As CEO of the UIATF, Bernard gained the respect of five governors of the state of Washington. He had friends and supporters in both houses of Congress in Washington, D.C. The last four mayors of Seattle were close to Bernard and supported his aims.

In 1995, Bernard was appointed to the board of directors of the National Museum of the American Indian in Washington, D.C. The board of directors was made up of the top spokesman and leaders of many tribes, who were selected to ensure quality and traditionalism in the creation and construction of the museum. The museum is to occupy the last six acres of the Smithsonian complex, opposite the East Wing Art

Museum and close to the Capitol. It will be a beautiful showplace for the creative accomplishments of all tribes in the United States. The museum is scheduled to open soon after 2002.

In 1996, Bernard and the UIATF were in the process of planning the People's Lodge. This large structure will house the Hall of Ancestors, the Potlatch House, a theater, and a museum. It will be a meeting place for Indians and visitors and also an educational facility for all who want to learn about the history and present directions of Indian tribes.

Seattle city officials approved a Pacific Northwest Indian Canoe Center, which will be administered by the UIATF. The center is part of the overall design of the south end of Lake Union. Carved ceremonial canoes will be anchored in the water alongside the exhibition center, both for display and for use by visitors who wish to ride in them.

On November 1, 1997, citizens, Indians, and friends representing various minority groups such as Chicanos, Asians, and blacks in Seattle held an appreciation banquet for Bernard. Everyone knew he had been diagnosed with incurable cancer. The banquet was a tribute to a man who had helped many. It was a celebration to acknowledge Bernard's commitment not only to the many tribes in Seattle but also to other minority associations in need of help.

Hundreds of people attended the event. Hattie Kauffman of *Good Morning, America* in New York served as emcee. Two governors of the state, Mike Lowry and Gary Locke, attended, as did Mayor Paul Schell of Seattle and U.S. Representative James McDermott. Others from city and state government were also there. Senator Patty Murray prepared and presented a Certificate of Achievement, and Donna Shalala, the Secretary of the Department of Health and Human Services, sent a Citation of Merit from Washington, D.C. Vine Deloria, the respected writer and educator from Boulder, Colorado, sent a letter stating that Bernard had done much for Indian people in the United States. The letter went on to describe Bernard as one of the truly great men of this century.

Daniel Evans, the former governor and senator from Washington, appeared on TV a few weeks later. He stated that Bernard had improved the lives of thousands of Indians. He went on to say that Bernard began his efforts in an era when it was not popular to try to change the status quo and added that because of this, he regarded Bernard as his personal hero.

Governor Locke declared November 1997 Bernard Whitebear Month to a standing ovation and then named Bernard First Citizen of the Decade in Washington State.

During February 2000, after months of fighting his illness, Bernard's condition worsened. A few weeks later, he was unable to work regularly. He had to direct his staff by telephone from his bedroom. His doctor thought it best to take him off chemotherapy because he wanted Bernard's last days to be comfortable.

Staff at the Daybreak Star Center brought Bernard's closest friend, Star, a large German shepherd, for one last visit. It was a special and touching stay as Star sat quietly by Bernard's side. The two seemed to communicate without talking.

On July 14, Bernard said his last words to Luana and me as we stood by his bedside. He was having difficulty breathing and uttered weakly, "I think this is it." We watched as he struggled to live. On July 16, 2000, after battling cancer for more than three years, Bernard Whitebear crossed over to the spiritual world. At 12:30 in the afternoon, while Luana and I were with him in his bedroom, he simply stopped breathing. I believe something inside Luana and me died that day. An era had ended for us.

A close friend of Bernard, Therese Kennedy Johns, wrote in a sympathy card, "He not only taught the art of living but the art of dying as well. I have never witnessed anyone die with so much grace."

On the evening of July 20, the Seven Drums performed at the wake in the Daybreak Star Center. The drums were there to help Bernard cross over. It was a solemn affair, and we could feel the spirits everywhere. Hundreds of Bernard's friends were there with him until sunrise.

The next morning, an escort of eight friends on Harley-Davidsons and sixteen motorcycle officers from the Seattle Police Department led the way to the Convention Center in downtown Seattle, followed by the hearse carrying Bernard and a throng of family and friends in cars. The memorial was held at 10:00 A.M. More than 2,500 people attended. Many from city, country, and state government were there. Numerous representatives of at least fifty-four tribes came to pay tribute. Senator Patty Murray, Senator Daniel Inouye, Governor Gary Locke, King County Executive Ron Sims, Mayor Paul Schell, Representative Jay Inslee, and former governor Mike Lowry spoke, praising Bernard as a friend and a champion for human rights. Humorous and thoughtful stories were shared. Governor Locke stated that he had erred in 1997 when he declared Bernard Whitebear First Citizen of the Decade. He said Bernard was a giant of a man and truly the First Citizen of the Century.

The U.S. flag at Fort Lawton was lowered to half-mast. At the end of the memorial, after taps, Mike Penney and six other Nez Perce sang and drummed the beautiful "Old Warrior's Song." This was the final tribute to a man who had fought hard battles, helped thousands, and lived his life well.

That night, hundreds of dancers assembled for the grand entry at the powwow on the Great Circle near the Daybreak Star Center. At the first drumbeat from the lead drum, lightning flashed, and thunder rocked the sky above. Large raindrops fell for a few seconds, and then the sky cleared abruptly. Many understood and regarded it as a signal from Bernard to let all of us know he was there.

Fifty-five years after Luana, Bernard, and I first came to Okanogan, I returned. The month was July, and the weather was hot. Okanogan had been a thriving town when our family came to work and live there in 1944. Now it has diminished in size and population. It looks like a town struggling to survive. Some of my favorite stores have closed. The Avalon Theatre no longer shows movies; it has been converted to another purpose. The once gracious Caribou Inn Hotel has suffered neglect and is probably beyond repair.

The attitudes of the people on both sides of the river have softened only a little over the years. There are still negative feelings on both sides, and their basic differences remain. They are still far apart on their attitudes toward the water, the land, and the beings that live off the land.

Luana, Bernard, and I tried to live with and overcome these differences. We had to straddle cultures to survive. We now accept that the Sin-Aikst Tribe and its culture are history. We see that the great homeland, once beautiful and still revered, has been defaced as a result of its occupation by others. We are aware that the Columbia River, once the greatest living force in the Northwest, is now a lifeless body of water. The great salmon are gone, and we still grieve their loss. The Sin-Aikst are called Lakes now, and it is not the same.

In 1956, the provincial government in Canada declared the Sin-Aikst Tribe extinct in British Columbia. That government fails to understand and admit that a number of Sin-Aikst live and make their homes in British Columbia with the Okanogan and the Shuswap. They do not recognize that hundreds of Lakes Indians, the direct descendants of the Sin-Aikst, live on the Colville Indian Reservation and in other parts of the world.

Some of the difficulties and humiliation we experienced have dimmed over the years. We met the challenges before us and overcame them one by one and from day to day.

The good people who taught and cared for Luana, Bernard, and me have crossed over. Our dad, Julian, died in a fire at his house in Malott in 1968. It is still unclear what started the fire and why he was unable to save himself. Our mother, Mary, lies peacefully at Pia, after her car accident in 1978. Harry Wong died of a stroke in Seattle in 1982. Our friends,

Brownie, Snooks, and the squirrel, have also crossed over, and we believe they are with our first friend, Pickles.

Between 1942 and 1948, Harry and my mother brought four children into this world: Lotus, Harry Jr., Teresa, and Laura. Lotus died of pneumonia in Tacoma in 1943, when she was only a year old. My mother took the death very hard. Harry Jr., Teresa, and Laura now live in Seattle. In 1968 and 1969, Laura had two sons, David and Marland. Harry Jr. had a daughter, Adrienne, in 1990.

The years in Western Washington were better for Luana, Bernard, and me. We were fortunate to have the opportunity to work with good people—white, minority, and Indian—to improve the quality of life for Indians and others in the Seattle area. We were able to combine the strengths of our inherited culture with the knowledge we had acquired in the white man's world.

Throughout our years, we remained close in spirit with our grandfather, White Grizzly Bear. His spiritual presence always guided us. We inherited his love of the Sin-Aikst way, the Columbia River, Kettle Falls, and the salmon. We learned to respect all beings of the forest, as he did. Through him, we shared the dedication, loyalty, and love of family.

Although he crossed over to the spirit world years ago, we still felt his presence, wherever we were. His spirit and strength of character were always important to us. When we thought of him, it was with appreciation and pride. His love of the beings of the forest and the water inspired and guided my art. They are always the principal subjects of my work. We understood and appreciated that he was the last in our family to live as a true Sin-Aikst.

The same old masonry bridge still spans the Okanogan River. It still reaches for both sides of the river. In 1944, it was hard for us to cross it. Looking back, we see that by crossing it, new worlds were opened to us. In those new worlds, we were able to grow, combine our talents, and overcome obstacles in keeping with the beliefs of our forebears and the traditions of the People.

"History will judge those who have destroyed our culture and our rights. We have to value our culture, and the outside world has to respect that cultural right."—Miguel Puwainchir and Felipe Tsankush, Shuar Indians, Ecuador

RESOURCES

Adams, David Wallace. *Education for Extinction: American Indians and the Boarding School Experience, 1875–1928.* Lawrence: University Press of Kansas, 1995. The book provides a clear picture of the Chemawa Indian School from its beginnings to the present day. It presents the philosophy and reasons why Chemawa and other off-reservation Indian boarding schools were designed to diminish and destroy all feelings of being Indian. The book describes how the makeup and characteristics of different tribes were taken away, leaving Indians at a much lower level than the whites.

Chance, David H. *People of the Falls.* Kettle Falls, Idaho: Kettle Falls Historical Center, 1986. The book provides information on the earliest days of the Sin-Aikst at Kettle Falls. It describes how the Colvilles (Swhy-ayl-puh) and Lakes (Sin-Aikst) Tribes quickly lost their way of life and religion, independence, land, and fishery. White settlers took away furs, minerals, and finally, the land itself. The book shares stories of Coyote, Mole, Salmon, and Rattlesnake. It delves into the complexity and depth of Sin-Aikst thinking and their closeness to the beings around them. I learned in greater detail about the Sin-Aikst religion of the spirit powers, a religion I embrace today.

Lakin, Ruth. *Kettle River Country: Early Days along the Kettle River.* Orient, Wash.: Lakin, 1976. The book presented information on how the Sin-Aikst used roots and plants for food, medicine, and other purposes. It includes photographs of my relatives and friends who have crossed over. This brought back memories of stories of the Sin-Aikst that were passed down to my mother.

Miller, Jay, ed. *Mourning Dove: A Salishan Autobiography.* Lincoln: University of Nebraska Press, 1990. The book helped me understand in greater depth the Sin-Aikst feeling regarding spirit powers. It presents a clear picture of how the Sin-Aikst lived from birth to death, describing in detail how the young were prepared to live within the tribe, to accept its laws, customs, religion, and respect for family. Preparation of the body for burial after crossing over into the spiritual world is clearly explained.